BRUCE McLAREN

Other books by the same author:

Against All Odds
(co written with James Hunt, 1977)

Patrick Stephens Limited, an imprint of Haynes Publishing, has published authoritative, quality books for more than a quarter of a century. During that time the company has established a reputation as one of the world's leading publishers of books on aviation, maritime, motor cycle, car, motorsport, and railway subjects. Readers or authors with suggestions for books they would like to see published are invited to write to: The Editorial Director, Patrick Stephens Limited, Sparkford, Nr Yeovil, Somerset BA22 7JJ.

BRUCE McLAREN

THE MAN AND HIS RACING TEAM

Eoin S. Young

Foreword by Ron Dennis

Patrick Stephens Limited

First published by Eyre & Spottiswoode in 1971
This facsimile reprint, with additional material,
is published by Patrick Stephens Ltd in 1995

British Library Cataloguing-in-Publication Data:
A catalogue record for this book is available from the British Library.

ISBN: 1 85260 511 1

Library of Congress catalogue card no. 94 73833

Patrick Stephens Limited is an imprint of Haynes Publishing, Sparkford, Nr Yeovil, Somerset BA22 7JJ.

Printed in Great Britain by
Butler & Tanner Ltd, London and Frome

For Bruce – to whom I owe so much

'The news that he had died instantly was a terrible
shock to all of us, but who is to say that he had
not seen more, done more and learned more in his
twenty-six years than many people do in a lifetime?
To do something well is so worthwhile that to die
trying to do it better cannot be foolhardy. It would
be a waste of life to do nothing with one's ability,
for I feel that life is measured in achievement, not
in years alone.'

*Bruce McLaren writing on the death
of his team-mate Timmy Mayer*

Contents

Foreword by Ron Dennis, Managing Director of McLaren International

I was in Formula 1 when Bruce McLaren was racing, but I never met him. In those days I was a racing mechanic working with Cooper, followed by Brabham, and my involvement with the McLaren team only began a few years after Bruce's death. In retrospect I wish we had met, because I understand he was a great and intuitive engineer, an extremely competent driver, and a very dedicated individual.

It is difficult to equate Bruce's philosophy then with ours now. His was right for the time because it was a period of innovation. For example, the aerodynamic influence on Grand Prix cars was in its infancy then and the emphasis was very much on engines and reliability, weight, and safe, sound engineering practices. Today we're into aerospace technologies with a more exacting scientific approach and a need to know exactly what's taking place on the car at any one moment. Consequently there is a great use of sophisticated electronics.

It's interesting to wonder how Bruce would have coped with these advances. If you look at some of the more mature engineers and designers in Grand Prix racing, they have adapted to a degree, but the majority of them have really rejected electronics technology and still have their roots in the old rule-of-thumb approach. I wouldn't like to guestimate how Bruce would have coped with today's technology, but he had an engineering background and I'm sure he would have stayed with the pace.

The team was about 45 strong when I arrived, and the base was in Colnbrook. Shortly after the formation of McLaren International we moved down to Woking to a substantially larger and more modern factory. That was a big step forward, but nowhere near as big as our move to the new facilities in Woking Business Park. We have approximately 220,000 sq ft of factory space housed in seven units, the largest of which holds the McLaren Grand Prix team. This is around 80,000 sq ft, with a staff of 220. Within the Group we now employ 550 people, a figure which will rise quite dramatically over the next few years with new projects. We're very focused on the future. We need to improve our Grand Prix performance. We will be competitive sooner rather than later . . .

I'm often asked why I didn't change the name of the team, but while I don't want this to appear as a detrimental remark about Bruce, branding a company with your own name tends to be rather ego-driven. I think it stemmed from a need to develop credibility, but it's a thing of the past. I like to think that the McLaren brand name is now greater and stronger than any one individual, and I would certainly like that to be the case as far as I am concerned personally.

I am still in close contact with Bruce's mother and sisters, and two or three letters pass between us each year. They are obviously very pleased that the brand name has lived through the changes that McLaren has seen.

McLaren cars have won 104 GPs to become the most successful team in Formula 1 history, a record achieved by 11 different drivers, and using three different makes of engine. I work on the simple principle that if you win all the races you inevitably win the championship. We've won a lot of races, but as far as I'm concerned we haven't won enough. The key to continuous success is to realise that the recipe for success is constantly changing. The formula for success changes on a month to month basis, and it's the ability to adapt which sorts the men from the boys.

I'm not actually all that fussed about statistics. I don't think they're critical to the future. They give us a buzz at the time but they tend to record the past, not predict the future. They try to support the future by extrapolating numbers, but in reality we're all in control of our own destiny, and the management of our company controls the stability of the team for the future.

This is a business about humans, and all I do is try to give the humans who form the nucleus of McLaren the best tools to do their jobs. These range from the hardware in the factories through to the drivers who race the cars, to the budget that I provide them. This is my task, and hopefully I do it better than most.

I would say that my role within the Group is very much business-orientated. I'm not screwing the cars together, or determining the shape of the under-body – I'm responsible for the car's performance as regards the end result, but that is from being at the ship's helm. When it comes to the business success of the Group it is very much my responsibility. I therefore get a bigger kick from that because I'm more directly involved.

I'm the salesman, I'm the person who is selling the wares of McLaren, and those wares have to include a successful team/car/driver package. The task of selling is that much easier when there is success, so EVERYBODY plays a role in the future. Everybody plays a role in either the achievements of the team in winning races, or of the company as regards its profitability or its managerial successes. There is no one individual who should be able to take the credit – we're a team at McLaren.

Woking, 1995

Preface

Bruce always felt that credit should go to his racing team – 'I would like to think they couldn't do it without me, but I know I certainly couldn't have done it without them' – and for that reason I have written this portrait of the McLaren team, setting the scene with Bruce's career to help the reader understand why the other members of the team who are introduced later could be carried along by the infectious McLaren enthusiasm for work and success.

I am indebted to Denny Hulme, Teddy Mayer, Phil Kerr, Tyler Alexander, Robin Herd, Gordon Coppuck, Colin Beanland, Ron Smith and George Bolthoff for taking the time to talk with me about their special departments in the team and remembering what it was like working with Bruce. Thanks also to Ken Tyrrell, Peter Agg, Roy Lunn, Jim Kaser and all the others who helped me compile the various sections of the book with anecdotes and details that I had either forgotten or never knew.

I was one of the first directors of Bruce McLaren Motor Racing Limited when the company was formed late in 1963 and I had started working with Bruce as his secretary in 1962. In those early days we made up company procedure as we went along. Bruce used to say that we were a two-man act – he was the nice guy and I was the baddie. If deliveries were late or other problems had arisen it was my job to telephone the offender and deliver a verbal caning. That was when Bruce stepped in to smooth things over, apologize for his secretary's wrath, and by being his natural 'nice guy' self we inevitably succeeded in getting instant delivery, or satisfaction, and the person on the other end of the 'phone would hang up wondering what an extraordinarily nice chap like Bruce could be doing employing a swine like me. . . .

We worked together on his regular magazine articles for *Autosport* in England and we syndicated these features to other magazines and to newspapers in New Zealand. It reached the stage eventually where Bruce became so polished on the tape recorder that he virtually dictated the story just as it appeared in the magazine without the need for any tidying-up by me. If the tape was done while he was in the bath there were splashes, muffled exclamations, and giggles interspersed with his report. On occasions he would tape the story as he drove to work in his Mercedes and he would add a running commentary on the dozy habits of some of the other commuters. I never ceased to be amazed at the way Bruce could find words and descriptions for his experiences that were always so much better than I could have managed, and yet I was supposed to be the writer!

I left McLaren Racing in 1966 to start my own business as a freelance racing journalist and a racing consultant and I worked closely with Bruce and the team in both these areas.

Bruce never seemed unduly worried about time, particularly if he was engrossed in working on a new car at the factory, and it was not until the staff started to expand that he came to realize that not everyone lived and breathed racing; that some people had a life of their own to lead outside motorsport. It always seemed to be easier to work long hours when the boss was there beside you – and this often made it more difficult to leave before he did. As a driver, however, Bruce was often ordered to bed the night before a race. On one famous occasion in 1967 when the new M6A CanAm car had won three races in a row, Bruce made the mistake of mentioning in front of Tyler Alexander that their success did not really seem all that hard to achieve. 'Hard . . .?' Tyler queried with an incredulous look. 'I didn't see you in the garage at four o'clock this morning!'

The fact that Bruce was the same age, or younger, than many of the people in his team helped to start the tremendous sense of family loyalty that made the McLaren team easily the most cheerful when you looked down almost any pit lane on any track in Europe or America. Bruce and Denny Hulme were like brothers.

When I walked into the offices of *Autocar* just after lunch on June 2 this year and Martin Lewis told me he had heard on the radio that Bruce had been killed at Goodwood, I simply did not believe him. It took hours for the terrible reality to sink in, and then I realized that for years I had regarded him as a brother too. It was that sort of loss. He had introduced me to the European racing world, and I was very much aware that I owed whatever success I had achieved since I left the team solely to Bruce. But he was such a larger-than-life person that now it would not surprise me at all if he walked round the corner and said 'Hi.' That helps to make this book easier to write.

I want to thank particularly Frederick Muller Ltd, publishers of Bruce's original book *From the Cockpit*, for allowing me to quote passages here; also Simon Taylor, the Editor of *Autosport*, for allowing me to quote from Bruce McLaren's regular column; and the authors of *Autocourse* and *Grand Prix Racing Facts and Figures* for their reams of historical facts. Any errors that occur are my fault, not theirs.

This book would not have been possible without the support of Patty McLaren, help from Bruce's mother and father in New Zealand, and the ceaseless cups of coffee from my wife Sandra as I have been typing the manuscript at home in East Horsley.

Bruce was a great friend to so many people all over the world that I would like to think this book is a tribute from them to him, and perhaps it will help Bruce's international friends to know what made him the way he was, and what made his racing team so successful. If I have done that, I have succeeded.

EOIN S. YOUNG

East Horsley
December 23, 1970

Author's Introduction to the 1995 facsimile reprint

Motor racing is a capricious business that demands total commitment. It makes or breaks people and teams on a relentless on-going basis. Ron Dennis is one of the men that it made, and yet he is reluctant to claim his due. He suggests that putting your own name on is somehow politically incorrect, an old-fashioned vanity. This does not seem to have held back Williams or Benetton. Or is he right for different reasons? Bernie Ecclestone was once asked by journalist Alan Henry why he didn't change the name of the Brabham team when he bought it. 'If you and I went into partnership and bought Marks & Spencer,' replied Ecclestone, 'we'd hardly want to change the name to Ecclestone & Henry, would we?' And I suppose Ron might be reluctant to re-name his racing car Dennis when there is an old company of the same name in nearby Guildford famous for making lumbering commercial vehicles.

The name doesn't always guarantee success, any more than reputations sustain themselves in racing. The adage about being only as good as your last race result is famous for keeping generations of racing people on their toes. Two of Bruce McLaren's main rivals were Jack Brabham's team, and Colin Chapman's Team Lotus, but both have gone to the wall.

After Bruce's death the McLaren team gathered itself and set about re-grouping. Teddy Mayer and Phil Kerr continued in management and Tyler Alexander stepped into a stronger role on the engineering side. Denny Hulme would lead the driving team and other drivers would be signed, but the 'family' air had gone and it was now more of a business. It had to be.

Mayer's greatest coup was to sign 1972 World Champion Emerson Fittipaldi away from Lotus for the 1974 season and in an unprecedented move to snare several major sponsors at once, at a time when keeping ONE major backer was regarded as an achievment. The team had been sponsored by the cosmetics company Yardley but in the re-arrangement they were moved to one side as sole sponsors of a McLaren for Mike Hailwood. The 'A' team turned out in the combined livery of Marlboro and Texaco, with Emerson Fittipaldi joining Denny Hulme. Emerson won his second world title that summer and Denny retired.

In 1976 Fittipaldi decided to form a team of his own and McLaren were lucky to find James Hunt unemployed. Together they won the world title in 1976, but all was not well within. The success of '76 ebbed into lethargy and the team was sliding away, its competitive edge apparently lost. In 1980 Marlboro engineered a buy-in which would eventually put Ron Dennis and his designer John Barnard in control.

Phil Kerr went home to New Zealand. Mayer and Alexander stayed on, eventually leaving what had been 'their' team to pursue interests elsewhere in racing. Mayer joined the Penske Indycar team and is still with them. Alexander worked for various teams before re-joining McLaren as manager of Special Projects. Denny Hulme suffered a heart attack and died at the wheel of a BMW in a touring car race in Australia in 1992.

And the 'new' McLaren team? Up seemed to be the only direction. World Championships for Niki Lauda (1984), Alain Prost (1985-86-89) and Ayrton Senna (1988-90-91) all in Marlboro-McLarens, and a quarter of a century after Bruce's death, the team he gave his name to is still at the forefront of Formula 1.

It surely can't be 25 years since I walked into the editorial offices of *Autocar* that sunny afternoon in early June and Martin Lewis said 'Have you heard the news on the radio? Your mate's been killed at Goodwood . . .'

Eoin Young,
East Horsley, 1995

Introduction

Westhampnett aerodrome was one of a string of fighter bases along the south coast of England during the Battle of Britain.

Before the war it had been a quiet Sussex farm a couple of miles from Chichester and half a mile from the Goodwood horse racing course. When war threatened, the flat fields were taken over and landing strips were laid out, connected around the perimeter by taxi-ing and access roads. One of the Hurricane pilots who flew from Westhampnett was Squadron Leader Tony Gaze, an Australian serving with the Royal Air Force.

In 1946 when the fighting was over and there was time to think about motor sport again in England, Brooklands and Donington Park had gone, swallowed up by war factories. New tracks had to be found if racing was to be revived and it was then that Tony Gaze remembered the narrow strip of tarmac perimeter roads round Westhampnett. Gaze suggested the old fighter field, already becoming overgrown, to the Duke of Richmond and Gordon who owned the nearby Goodwood estate. The Duke had raced at Brooklands before the war as Freddie Richmond, the Earl of March, winning the 1930 B.R.D.C. 500 miles race in a little Ulster Austin Seven with Sammy Davis, and a year later he won the J.C.C. Double Twelve – a 24-hour race run in daylight over two days – driving an M.G. Midget with Chris Staniland.

It was with an Ulster Austin that Bruce McLaren learned about motor racing in New Zealand when he was fourteen. When he saw a large oil painting of an Ulster in action he bought it and hung it in pride of place in his new home. It was of the Duke winning at Brooklands in 1930.

Wing Commander Tommy Wisdom, well known as a racing

driver and a journalist, was asked by the Duke for his opinion of Westhampnett as a possible motor racing venue and when Tommy endorsed Gaze's opinion, Goodwood was born.

The first race on the Goodwood circuit was in 1947 and the last was in 1966. The threat of high lap speeds from the new 3-litre Grand Prix cars would have meant costly modifications to the safety measures and the Duke decided to close the track. Racing stopped, but the lap speeds rose fantastically during private testing.

The grandstands, the pits, the covered paddock area, the control buildings, and the concrete-protected marshal's posts were left. . . .

Stirling Moss started his racing career with his first major drive in a Cooper 500 in 1948 at Goodwood and fourteen years later that sparkling career finished in the bank at St Mary's. He had been out to raise the lap record which John Surtees had set and Stirling had equalled earlier in the race at 1min 22sec (105.37mph). Stirling made a pit stop to check sticking throttles on the apple-green UDT-Laystall Lotus-Climax V8 and he was making up time when the car inexplicably lunged off the road into the bank and Stirling was lucky to escape with his life. He never raced again.

When the track finally closed the lap record stood to the two Flying Scots – Jim Clark and Jackie Stewart – in their 1.5 litre Lotus and BRM Formula 1 cars at 1min 20.4sec (107.46mph), but already in unofficial testing Bruce McLaren had lapped at 1min 17.2sec in one of his McLaren-Oldsmobile sports cars. Bruce loved Goodwood. He knew every inch of the 2.4 mile track. It was only an hour from his factory at Colnbrook, and the team always used Goodwood to try new cars and new developments.

In 1967 Dan Gurney and Jack Brabham were lapping at 1min 15.4sec in their formula 1 cars and that season Denis Hulme was down to 1min 13.4sec in the new M6A McLaren CanAm sports car. Three years later in the early summer of 1970, Bruce had lowered the test record to 1min 8.8sec (125.58

mph) with his newest sports car, the M8D which had been christened 'The Batmobile' because of the high side fins sloping up both sides of the tail with a wing slung between them. However the Goodwood lap record is now held by Denis Hulme at 1min 7.8sec.

Lap speeds in figures mean little more to the average reader than an earthquake death toll in Tibet, but to lap a track like Goodwood as a passenger in a CanAm sports car is to appreciate the difference between good racing drivers and mere mortals.

With 630 horsepower from the Chevrolet V8 engine bellowing in the back, the car accelerates down the pit lane. The aluminium engine is bolted to a plate directly behind the cockpit, acting as part of the chassis. Two hip-hugging seats are scooped into the aluminium riveted monocoque box that forms the frame of the car and accommodates 64 gallons of pump petrol stowed in bag tanks. Every ounce of the 1,420lb. car is purpose-built for pace. 6,500 revolutions per minute on the dial directly in front of the driver is 110mph in low gear. Up to 140mph in second and you are into the never-ending right-hander at Madgwick. The scenery starts to blur. Third and 175mph through the flat-out kink to the right at Fordwater. In top gear on a flying lap the car goes through this kink as fast as it does on the main straight. Back into third for St Mary's and flashing by on your left is the bank where Moss crashed. Foot hard on the floor down through the tricky left-hander at 115mph and you are charging at the sharp Lavant right-hander.

Lavant calls for delicate horsepower ballet as you grab second momentarily right on top of the corner. You are already hard on the brakes, but the lower gear snatches the rear tyres into an oversteering slide. The instant the car is aimed for the straight you whack it into third and surge away from the corner. A hundred yards away and you are into top at 130mph and still accelerating judderingly hard with the engine transmitting every ounce of power through the pair of rear Goodyears like rubber rollers fourteen inches across each flat tread. You use a lot of road through the slight left-hand kink out on to the straight proper because it is a kink that gets tighter the faster you go.

Woodcote, the right-hander at the end of the straight, looks as though it has been loaded into a cannon and fired at you point blank as the needle on the rev counter tremors up to six-six – 180mph. Suddenly the brakes arrest the car in full flight like a giant hand snatching you from certain destruction against the far bank. In the passenger's seat the G force of retardation is so powerful that your knees feel like they are slicing through the riveted dash panel. Woodcote is lined up and gone, the manoeuvre planned 100 feet before we arrived and executed automatically. At that speed your mind works at computer speed. Instantly there is a wall across the road. There is no hope of stopping but an arrow indicates salvation to the right and as you plunge at the wall a gap opens on the far side and you slither through with the exhaust bark bouncing off the walls. The relaxing of tension as the car swerves to the pits is beautiful.

A lap like that two-up from a standing start would have equalled the old lap record set by two of the fastest drivers in the world with Grand Prix cars!

After his tests with the prototype M8D which was to be driven on the CanAm series by Denny Hulme, Bruce flew to Indianapolis to oversee the running of the first McLaren entries in the '500', enthusing at the performance of the latest in the line of McLaren title-winning sports cars. Bruce had won the CanAm championship in 1967 and 1969 and Denny had filled the gap in 1968. The CanAm McLarens were unbeatable. They had won all eleven races in the Championship the season before, and Bruce was anxious to get back from Indianapolis to test the second car which he would drive on the 1970 Series.

The car was ready to run on the Tuesday after the '500', but the fibreglass body had not been completed so it was decided to fit Bruce's car with Denny's body for the tests.

Bruce arrived back from America on Monday, June 1, and the following morning he drove down to Goodwood in his 250SE Mercedes with Ron Smith, a friend who managed Patsy

Burt's sprint McLaren M3A and her garage at Bookham in Surrey. Ron had worked for Moss in the early days and he often helped the McLaren team by looking after management duties during test sessions. It was a test day like any other.

On the hour trip down Bruce told Ron about the various problems they had come up against at Indianapolis where Carl Williams had finished ninth and Peter Revson's McLaren had quit after 87 laps. Bruce confessed that it was a new world totally unlike Grand Prix racing, but he was bubbling over with new ideas for a 1971 Indianapolis McLaren.

It was a sunny June morning with a slight breeze across the airfield rippling the windsock. The Hurricanes and Spitfires scrambling from Westhampnett thirty years earlier had been replaced by leisurely light aircraft doing circuits-and-bumps.

A Formula 1 McLaren had been brought down as well as the new CanAm car, because Peter Gethin was to take Denny Hulme's place for the Belgian Grand Prix at Spa the next weekend and he had to get the cockpit tailored to fit. Denny was still recovering from burns received during practice at Indianapolis three weeks earlier.

Peter had not arrived and the CanAm car was being trundled around by New Zealand mechanic Cary Taylor who had raced a 1.5 litre Brabham at home before he came over to work for the Brabham team and later joined the McLaren CanAm crew. He was running the new car in, and had been chuntering around since nine o'clock making sure there were no leaks or other problems before Bruce got down to sorting it out at speed. Ron clocked a lap out of interest at 1min 28.4sec.

The Formula 1 car was sitting fuelled and ready to run, so Bruce decided to do a few laps in it. He came in after a best lap of 1min 12.2sec and waited for the CanAm sports car to have the brake balance adjusted and five gallons of fuel added. At 3.5mpg it was easier to keep adding fuel than to park out on the circuit with dry tanks. For testing the car ran with tanks only about a third full.

At 10.45 Bruce drove out of the pits for the first time in his

new car and after a standing lap and a flyer he was heading for
the pits. There was more high-speed oversteer than he liked and
he mentioned to Ron that the special steering wheel they had
made for the Indianapolis cars with a flattened bottom would
be better than the normal wheel with its fat leather-bound
round rim. It was more comfortable on the tops of the thighs
with a flattened rim in the wriggle-fit cockpit.

The mechanics raised the wing just a fraction to increase the
downthrust and try to curb the oversteer.

He went out again and after four laps, two of which equalled
his earlier time with the 3-litre Formula 1 car, he came back to
the pits to have the wing angle raised another notch. He said
the sports car felt a lot softer everywhere compared with the
precision of the open-wheeled Grand Prix car at the same speed
so the crew checked the fat Goodyears pressuring them at
22psi all round. They put tape under the front duct in the nose
to check the possibility of grounding, and as an efficient test
driver Bruce rattled off the instrument readings he had checked
coming down to Woodcote on the last lap. Oil temperature
90°C. Water temperature 70°C. Fuel pressure 140. Oil pressure
60.

Another four laps for a best of 1min 11.2sec and he was back
for a further notch on the wing. Taking advantage of the stop
they filled the tanks just to the top of the first layer of safety
foam. That made it about twenty gallons on board. Six laps
then for a best of 1min 10.8sec (122.03mph) and he reported
that the high-speed oversteer had been cured. Instead he now
had a trace of understeer. He was pulling only just over
6,400rpm on the straight and he wondered what had happened
to the other 200rpm. Perhaps he was losing time coming out of
Lavant on to the straight, so he asked for adjustments to the roll
bars front and rear. Another five laps to equal his previous
time and he came back to say that the handling was better and
he was back up to six-six again on the straight.

The oil temperature was up five degrees but the other
instruments were normal. They checked tyres and shock absor-

bers to see why it might be oversteering at Madgwick just after the pits.

At 12.19 by Ron's pit watch the big orange finned McLaren rumbled away down the pit lane. Another few laps and they would stop for lunch. All was well as Bruce twitched the tail coming out of the chicane and set off on the flyer.

He never completed the lap. At 12.22pm he was dead; killed instantly when the car left the road just after the left-hand kink on the main straight and slammed into a marshal's protective embankment on the right-hand side of the track. An investigation of the scattered wreckage showed that a section of the tail must have lifted at around 170mph causing immediate instability and a situation that was beyond human control.

1 Bruce McLaren's Early Life

Bruce Leslie McLaren was born in Auckland, New Zealand, on August 30, 1937, under the sign of Virgo, the craftsman. It was prophetic.

Ruth and Leslie McLaren were proud of their first son and second child, a brother for their seven-year-old daughter Patricia. Les McLaren had recently bought a service station and garage in the wealthy suburb of Remuera and their home was just round the corner in Upland Road. With his three younger brothers Les had helped to maintain something of a McLaren domination in local motorcycle sport and he was thinking of switching his enthusiasm to cars. 'Pop', as he was known to everyone later in the racing world, may have known that in Europe during that August, Mercedes W125s had won the Grands Prix of Monaco and Germany and that Ernst von Delius had been killed at the Nurburgring when his Auto Union crashed on the straight, but he certainly would never have imagined that twenty-one years hence his infant son would make his name in international racing on the Nurburgring and that in twenty-five years' time he too would win the Grand Prix round the streets of Monaco.

After the war, Les sold his Singer Le Mans sports car and bought a 1935 SS I – the forerunner of the Jaguar – ostensibly because the larger car would help to accommodate the fifth member of the McLaren family, Janice who was born in 1947. The sporty SS also served as a competition mount and Les competed in sprint events and beach races. To have a racing driver as a father must have been good value at school where Bruce was captain of the juniors' rugby football team, and like most husky young New Zealanders Bruce dreamed of being an 'All Black' and playing for his country.

He was nine and a half when the pains started in his left hip. A polio epidemic was sweeping the country and anxious mothers watched their children for any sign of an ache or pain. In fact Bruce had probably been so determined not to get polio that he never told his parents about the pain that was causing him to favour his left leg at school. Eventually the pain became too much even for the captain of the junior rugby team to ignore and his confession brought panic to the household at Upland Road.

An X-ray showed that the pains were due not to polio but to Perthes Disease which resulted in the virtual seizing up of the ball-and-socket hip joint. A fall could have caused the problem, but nobody, including Bruce, could ever be sure just which bump had caused it. Twelve months earlier on his uncle's farm at Ngaruawahia he had fallen from a horse and hit a fence post on his way to the ground. He had also been involved in a trolley smash in a race down a long hill in Remeura.

Whatever the cause, the result was a month in hospital and then almost three years in the Wilson Home for Crippled Children. There were very real fears that he might never walk again. His legs were encased in plaster casts and he lay on his back in traction for months. His tenth and eleventh birthdays came and went before he was allowed to leave his wheelchair and try walking on crutches. He said later that in his eagerness to get mobile again he pounded round the hospital grounds building the foundation to the broad shoulders that were to be so characteristic of him. The only lasting effect of the disease was a limp since his left leg was one-and-a-half inches shorter than the right and he wore a shoe with a built-up heel to compensate. He had kept up his schooling in the Wilson Home, and he spent a year at home taking correspondence courses before he was allowed to face the hurly-burly of school once again in 1951. Rugby, basketball and other contact sports had been ruled out by the doctors, so Bruce instead took up rowing.

By the end of his first year on the engineering course at Seddon Memorial Technical College he was heading his class in applied mechanics, chemistry and engineering shopwork.

At this stage it might have been mentioned over lunch in the McLaren kitchen that perhaps it was not such a good idea to be using the family car for weekend competition, and with three growing children Les could understand the position. He decided to buy a car that he could use purely for racing, and to this end he tracked down an Ulster Austin Seven. The car had seen better days but it was a racing car, albeit a 1929 one, and in remote New Zealand this resulted in a price tag of £110 for the stripped car. The previous owner had pulled the car down to give it a complete rebuild but had lost heart. Parts of the car were starting to rust in boxes where they had been carefully placed for hopeful reassembly. The enormity of the task he was undertaking must have come to Pop on the way home as the little chassis swayed at the end of the tow rope and his twelve-year-old son sat among the boxes of bits and pieces on the back of the workshop truck wondering if his father really knew what he was letting himself in for.

The rebuild took a year. Since replacement parts for the 1929 racing Austin were unobtainable Les made do with second hand standard Austin Seven parts which he modified to fit. After work in the evenings and at weekends Les always had an eager watcher cum helper in Bruce as the Ulster finally took some sort of shape. Even when it was finished the car was scarcely impressive, but it was hand-built, reborn, and since his father had performed this mechanical miracle there was not a better racing car around as far as Bruce was concerned.

The Ulster was elegant in a miniature sort of way, but almost ridiculous when you compare the specifications with the sports cars that Bruce was to build under his own name later. The tiny 747cc 4-cylinder engine had an aluminium crankcase with a 56mm bore and a 76mm stroke. The compression ratio was six to one and at 5,000rpm it developed 24bhp. Oil pressure seldom rose above five pounds.

It had a three-speed gearbox with factory quoted speeds of 28mph in first, 50mph in second and 72mph in top. Suspension was by a semi-elliptic spring across the front, with cord-bound quarter elliptics at the rear. Steering was by worm and wheel. The spidery wire wheels were 19 inches in diameter. The wheelbase was 6ft. 3in., track was 3ft. 4in. and the whole car weighed about 950 pounds.

In England the Ulster Austins had put up formidable performances in their class, and a very young Bruce McLaren was to learn the basics of racing in the tiny cockpit.

When the Great Day arrived and Les fired the little engine for the first time, Bruce eagerly awaited his father's report at the end of his first test run down the road. He could hardly believe it when his father returned shaken to say that far from behaving like a Grand Prix car, it was almost uncontrollable. The steering was lamentable, the brakes were a joke, it handled like nothing on earth and the first thing he was going to do was place an advertisement in the *Auckland Star* to sell it. Bruce was appalled. He pleaded with his father and eventually won his case. The Ulster could stay providing Bruce maintained it himself. He had more than a year to wait until he could go for his driving licence, but Les was obviously well aware that he was providing Bruce with the best possible way of gaining practical experience in engineering.

He booked a driving test days after his fifteenth birthday and borrowed a friend's Morris Minor to get his licence. Next on the McLaren list of motoring ambitions was his first competition event and this turned out to be a hillclimb at Muriwai, about twenty-five miles from Auckland and close to the beach where the McLaren family had a weekend home. Some of the early beach races had been held on the Muriwai sands and Bruce never forgot this important link in his career. When, a few months before his death, he bought a new luxury home in Burwood Park near Walton-on-Thames in Surrey he named the house 'Muriwai'.

Les McLaren was in hospital when Bruce made his first

BRUCE MCLAREN'S EARLY LIFE · 31

competition appearance on the shingle hill, but he had issued
stern instructions to try and curb his son's enthusiasm. That
evening Bruce visited his father in hospital with the news that he
had won his class with a best climb of 72 seconds and beaten
another kid called Phil Kerr who was racing an Austin Nippy.

Phil Kerr, later to become Jack Brabham's manager and
eventually joint managing director of Bruce's racing team in
England, had heard about Bruce and his Ulster through friends
at school. 'There was a competitive element prior to the hillclimb because I think we were both wondering how good the
other one was and what sort of car he had. This was on a very
junior scale, I must admit, but nevertheless there was a definite
competitive element.'

From then on Bruce and Phil were allowed to work on their
Austins in the McLaren garage, with Pop or the shop foreman
Harold Bardsley always prepared to aid with advice but not
with assistance. They reasoned that it was better to explain to
the boys how the job should be done and let them do it, rather
than to move in and do the job for them. They were right. With
the urge for competition upon him and the pressing need to stay
faster than Phil, Bruce moved ahead with modifications on the
Ulster. The car had arrived on 19-inch wheels and these were
replaced with 16-inch disc wheels on the rear and 17-inch wires
on the front. The rear springs were flattened to cope with the
oversteer, and the front spring was turned upside down to lower
the car but when the king pins started to chew out, a front axle
from an Austin Big Seven was fitted and the problem was solved.

The single Zenith carburettor had been replaced by twin
SUs on a McLaren-built manifold and Bruce's times up the
Muriwai hill had been clipped to 47 seconds. This was enough
to keep Phil behind him while he was driving his own Nippy,
but Bruce was less than impressed the day he loaned Phil the
Ulster and Phil equalled the McLaren times. . . . In 1958 when
the 'Driver to Europe' scheme first started, the three names to
choose from were Bruce, Phil and a friend of theirs, Merv Mayo.

During 1954 when perhaps more effort was being put in on

the Austin than on homework, Bruce's marks at Seddon Tech started to slump and there were some terse teachers' comments on the end-of-term reports, but in his final year during 1955 he was back on top of the class again and was a school prefect as he had been for the past couple of years.

In January that year Bruce saw his first major race when New Zealand staged its first Grand Prix and Bruce and Phil were crowd marshals. 'We took the easy way out,' Bruce remembered in *From the Cockpit*. 'We sat down to watch the race while the crowd behind happily sorted themselves out.'

Until this time Bruce and his father had been sharing drives in the Ulster but late in 1954 Les bought one of the first production Austin Healey 100s in the country which had been raced by Ross Jensen. Preparation of the two Austins continued side by side, with the Ulster now tuned enough to be unsuitable for driving to school – by parental decree. When the cylinder head cracked on the Ulster, Bruce set about making a new one using a head from a 1936 Austin Ruby saloon, filling the combustion chambers with bronze and carving them out again with a rotary file. The new head was a success as Bruce proved returning regular times under 20 seconds for a quarter mile, with a terminal velocity of 87mph through the flying quarter.

In August 1955, with university looming the following year, Bruce decided to sell the Ulster and buy a car he could use on the road and compete in as well. With £280 from the sale of the Ulster and £30 that he had borrowed, he invested in a Ford Ten Special but he was never happy with the car and was relieved when the opportunity came to race his father's Healey instead.

The McLaren-Kerr struggle advanced from the Austin Seven class up to the Ford Ten category since Phil had bought a Buckler sports car and another friend, Colin Beanland, had a tuned-up Anglia saloon. Colin was to accompany Bruce to England in 1958 while Phil continued his accountancy studies, and several years later Colin rejoined the McLaren team, eventually settling in America as manager of McLaren Engines Inc., in Detroit.

Bruce started work on an engineering degree out at Auckland University's engineering college at Ardmore near where the first Grand Prix races were held. He was passing all his subjects, but he was having to apply himself more as the work intensified and he had less time to work on his cars. It must have occurred to him that he might be better off to leave and work in his father's business (which would also mean more time to work on his cars) but he continued at university.

Pop had entered the Healey in the sports car race prior to the 1956 Grand Prix but when doctor's orders, following a spell in hospital, made it apparent that he would not be able to make use of his entry, Bruce begged his father to let him take his place. Gearbox trouble in practice meant Bruce's first all-nighter before the race and a blown head gasket caused his retirement but he slept through the Grand Prix later in the afternoon happy in the knowledge that he had driven in his first major race. And one of his competitors had been Stirling Moss in a Porsche! As Pop's health improved they struck a family bargain whereby whoever was faster in practice would drive the Healey in the race. At the time this must have seemed like a fair bargain since Pop's experience could presumably be relied on to counter Bruce's exuberance. That was when the talent started to show through. On the Ohakea airfield circuit where Bruce had raced the Ulster previously, he was seven seconds faster than his father in practice and their bargain was effectively scrapped. Pop concentrated on being team manager after that.

The following summer they planned to compete in all the international races with the Healey, which was getting faster and faster. The engine had been pulled down and fitted with Chrysler pistons and exhaust valves, and Buick cam followers. The ports were opened out and a special double exhaust system was fitted. A full-length under-tray helped top speed, and to compete with the disc-braked Healey 100S which was now being driven by Ross Jensen, the 100–4's drum brakes were ventilated with cooling holes and scoops on the back plates.

Ken Wharton's death, when his Monza Ferrari crashed in the

sports car race, took the edge off the start of the 1957 season at
Ardmore but Bruce finished fifth behind a D-type Jaguar, Jack
Brabham in a bob-tailed Cooper that Bruce was soon to buy, an
Australian special called an Ausca, and Ross Jensen in the 100S.
At Levin he was third, at Wigram a valve dropped through a
piston, he was third at Dunedin, but after a misfire on Inver-
cargill's Ryall Bush road circuit where the Healey was getting
up to 130mph, the engine finally poked a rod through the side.

Back in Auckland, Bruce returned to college at the beginning
of term and tried to take his mind off the broken Healey. That
was when the centre-seat bob-tailed 1½-litre Cooper that
Brabham had driven came on the market. The Healey and the
unloved Ford Special were sold to effect the deal that was
probably helped with a slice of Pop's savings. It was Bruce's
first Cooper drive and he revelled in the whole new scene. After
a couple of small events at the end of the summer the car was
completely stripped down to its tubular chassis. The McLaren
racing programme had now progressed well beyond Austin
Sevens and Ford Tens and Phil and Colin were able to do little
more than marvel at the detail on 'real' racing cars and weigh
in with a polishing rag on bodywork and magnesium rims.

With the Ford gone Bruce was pedalling his bicycle to college
and he was reaching the stage where he had to choose between a
career as a motor engineer or a civil engineer. It was really a
choice between working on engines or bridges and there seems
little doubt that he would have settled for the motor side if it
had been left to him. The 'Driver to Europe' scheme effectively
saved Bruce from the decision.

He had stayed in touch with Brabham by letter during the
year, sorting out the odd impenetrable problem that cropped up
with the sports car, and Jack suggested that a deal could be
arranged whereby he brought out a pair of single-seater Coopers
for the 1958 season in New Zealand, one to be driven by Bruce.
The sports car was sold to Merv Neil, the final university
examinations were over, and Bruce settled down to await the
arrival of the 1,750cc Cooper. He spent his spare time working

with Phil and Colin as they helped Merv Mayo complete his Buckler sports car, little knowing that the choice of 'Driver to Europe' was to lie between Bruce, Phil and Merv.

In fact his first real single-seater drive was at the wheel of a supercharged 3-litre Maserati 8CLT which had been built for Indianapolis but never raced there. The car had been bought from the estate of Freddie Zambucka by Frank Shuter who planned to try for the New Zealand speed record and Bruce's job was to make the Maserati a runner. He spent hours cleaning the jellified dope fuel out of the system, but the shattering bark of the exhaust when he finally fired it up was worth all the trouble. A track test at Ohakea was memorable for the abundance of power that brought wheelspin up to 140mph, and the vagaries of the handling. Bruce was impressed, but glad to hand the Maserati over to its new owner and get down to the Auckland wharves to check the unloading of the two Coopers, a 1,960cc Formula 1 car for Jack Brabham and a smaller 1,750cc Formula 2 car for himself.

After a few follow-my-leader laps on Jack's tail at Ardmore, Bruce was waved past and Jack sat in behind to see if his pupil had cottoned on to what he had been trying to teach in the previous laps. Bruce was rather nonplussed when Jack ticked him off later for hanging the tail out too much. That, he thought, was just a bit strong – especially coming from Brabham who used the tail-out oversteering slide as his trademark in the early Cooper days!

Following orders, he came home second in the first race heat on the morning of the Grand Prix at Ardmore, and with plenty of willing helpers he set about preparing the car for what was to be the race that launched him on his career. The rear of the car was raised on the quick lift jacks and Bruce was running the car with the rear wheels spinning so that the transmission and engine would be warmed up for the start. Nobody believed the clunk from the transmission – until the second clunk. Bruce switched off the engine and ran to tell Jack that something terrible had happened to the gearbox. There was less than half an hour to the start of the race when Jack arrived back lugging a spare transmission and the McLaren crew started desperately unbolting the broken gearbox to fit the new one. It seemed like an impossible task. The local organizers did their bit by delaying the start of the Grand Prix with a fake search for oil on the back of the circuit, but they finally had to put the grid under starter's orders and flag it away. Behind the pits the final bolts were being done up on the McLaren Cooper and while Bruce hastily buckled on his helmet, oil was dashed in, and he was wheelspinning his way out on to the grid to take up the chase. He had half a lap to make up.

Later in his career, Bruce was to repeat this ability to perform near miracles under stress. In a situation where last-minute problems had set him back, or if he was angered, he could turn on fantastic performances. At Mosport in Canada in 1967 a leaking fuel bag in his M6A CanAm sports car delayed his start and he set off fifty seconds after the field. He fought his way through the pack to second place behind his team-mate Denny Hulme. In 1963 he brought one of the first Downton-prepared Mini Coopers to New Zealand and he qualified it on pole position for the saloon race. Just before the start he was told that he would have to start from the back of the grid because the drivers of some of the larger-engined cars had protested that they would run the little Cooper down before the first corner. Irate, Bruce drove like a man possessed, threaded his way to the front of the field in two laps and led the race until overheating slowed him to second behind a 3.8 litre Jaguar.

It was difficult to arouse Bruce, but when his fuse was lit he was very definitely hot property!

At Ardmore in 1958 he must have felt near to tears when the transmission clattered so close to the start of the Grand Prix, but the urgency of the chase overtook him and when he drove out on the track he was the local hero out to make good. He was up to eighth place when the engine started to misfire and he stopped to change the plugs. In his haste he had forgotten to change from the soft warm-up plugs they were using when the gearbox failed. Seven minutes dragged by as the plugs were changed and Bruce saw all his hard-earned placings being lost. He went back into the race a very lonely last but he was starting to get the feel of the car now that the heat was off, when the transmission started to tighten up and he called back at the pits. His race was over. The bellhousing studs had loosened, the oil had drained out, and the gears were ruined.

So, it seemed, were his chances of winning the 'Driver to Europe' scholarship. It looked as though a run of bad luck would ruin his big chance and he would have to resign himself to his engineering studies. So near and yet so far.

When it was announced that night at the prize-giving that despite his misfortunes that afternoon, Bruce was to be the first driver to be presented with the award from the New Zealand International Grand Prix Association of a trip to Europe with introductions to racing teams and a grant to cover expenses during the season, Bruce was stunned. The world started going round again.

He asked Colin Beanland if he would come with him as a sort of companion mechanic. When Colin protested that he was a clerk in a wholesale spare parts business and hardly a racing mechanic, Bruce smoothed it all out and said it would be simple to learn as he went along.

The McLaren entourage went south again that summer towing the Cooper behind the new 2.4 litre Jaguar, and despite a broken crownwheel at Wigram, he collected a pair of second places at Dunedin and Teretonga behind Ross Jensen in the 250F Maserati. Jensen was the winner of the New Zealand Gold Star that season and he really deserved it with immaculate drives in the 'Grey Lady', as the equally immaculate 250F was known. Ross, now running a flourishing BMW dealership in Auckland, had no peer on New Zealand tracks that season. It was at Teretonga that drifting sand caused odd traction problems similar to those at Zandvoort, which Bruce countered by fitting Michelin X road tyres to his Cooper!

Knowing that Bruce was competing in the hillclimb at

Clellands, some twenty miles from my hometown of Timaru, and would be staying with his sister Pat, now married to John Hunter who was manager of the local Lucas depot, I introduced myself at Teretonga and took full advantage of my new acquaintance with a top driver by billing him highly for the hillclimb in the preview I wrote for the *Timaru Herald*. I was then working in the Australia and New Zealand Bank and borrowing time on the bank's typewriter to tap out freelance columns on motoring for the local paper.

Bruce fell somewhat short of my estimation in the hillclimb because, after filling the Cooper's differential with plumber's lead to lock it, a halfshaft snapped on his second run and he ended the afternoon with a best time of 55.3sec which was worth a class win ahead of a Triumph TR2, but only third fastest of the day behind Morrie Stanton in the fearsome Stanton Special which had a supercharged Gypsy Moth aeroplane engine mounted amidships, and Dick Campbell in a Mark 9 Cooper 500. Further down the results it said that one E. Young (Austin A30) had finished second in class behind a Cooper-Anzani with a time of 62.9sec for the hill. It was the first and last time that my name appeared in the same list of results as Bruce McLaren's and my last competition appearance. Banking and later writing were far less wearing on the nerves and the pocket.

That night Bruce and I went down to the local dance in his father's Jaguar and I introduced him to Pat Broad. Bruce asked if he could escort her home but she explained that she was sorry but she was going on to a party. We toured Timaru that night trying to find the party but finally gave up. The next day I tracked down Pat's telephone number and Bruce called round to see her. They were engaged after the 1960 Grand Prix at Ardmore and in 1961 they were married in Christchurch.

Bruce had decided to take his 1,750cc Cooper to England with him and have the engine altered to comply with the 1,500cc Formula 2 regulations, and the car was shipped to Sydney for re-loading on the *Orantes* which would take it to London. Bruce and Colin flew to Sydney on March 15, 1958, trying to look a lot more confident than they felt in their new black blazers that had been presented to them with 'NZIGP Driver to Europe' emblazoned in silver letters under New Zealand's national emblem, the silver fern.

The *Orantes* stopped to load cargo in Melbourne and there was a letter waiting for Bruce to tell him that the NZIGP had arranged a start in a works Formula 2 Cooper at Aintree on April 15 which meant that he would have to leave the ship and fly to make it in time. He climbed down into the cargo hold and spent an hour removing his tailor-made clutch and brake pedals, the St Christopher medal from the dash panel and his helmet and goggles.

Once again Jack Brabham was looking after his New Zealand protégé and starting money of £60 had been arranged. Charles Cooper, wary of another of these bush lads arriving to drive his cars, stipulated that Bruce had to insure the car and after paying the premium of £50, he emerged with a paper profit from his first race. Problems with the Weber carburettors dropped him to ninth place in his first event 'abroad', but just being there was fuel for the twenty-year-old McLaren ego.

The latest Formula 2 Coopers had coil spring suspension so Bruce decided to sell his own car to Steve Ouvaroff and invest in one of the new Coopers. He had to build it himself in the workshops. When Colin arrived on the *Orantes*, he and Bruce took a room at the Royal Oak, the pub just round the corner from the Cooper factory but in fact backing on to the rear of the workshops across a little stream. A plank across the stream solved the distance to work problem, and they soon discovered that the saloon bar was more or less a Cooper clubhouse. They only paid rent on their room while they were actually there which was ideal as they were often away at races and they were not likely to get rich quickly on the starting money Bruce was earning. 'He didn't always win,' says Colin, 'but at least there was some money in the bank. This didn't stay there though because he wanted to improve the car and put disc brakes on it.'

That meant perhaps £90 for a set. And then the big thing was the limited-slip differential. All these things cost money and there were times when we ate spaghetti for days on end simply because we didn't have the money. Often we couldn't scrape up enough for my wages, but that didn't really matter because I was there for a look around and perhaps do a bit of racing. I bought a Mark I Zephyr to tow the Cooper and we borrowed a trailer from the factory.'

The idea of paying any form of retainer or expenses for a mechanic had not apparently occurred to the Grand Prix Association when they started the scholarship scheme, but it was an important item and one that was taken care of in future awards. 'You really had to have someone giving you a hand. You needed someone to give you pit signals. And when you're 12,000 miles from home and you're a 20-year-old kid, it's kind of handy just to have someone to talk to, if nothing else.' Colin knew the score.

There were plenty of lessons to be learned in that first year. When the production Cooper tube frames came off the chassis jigs, the wishbones were bolted on, the car was assembled by hand and this meant that each car was just a little bit different. Bruce and Colin were helping to put the finishing touches to a friend's Cooper when they realized that the wheels were pointing at some odd angles. They ran a string round the car and drew this to the owners' attention. Then it dawned on them that perhaps their own car was like this. It was. They solved the problem by welding washers on to the chassis lugs where the wishbones bolted on, until the car was set up perfectly. The next race was at Crystal Palace and Bruce went sailing backwards into a bank in the rain which did bad things to their precise setting-up. Oddly enough, according to Colin, this did not have a great deal of adverse effect on the handling so they were left to figure that either the Cooper was extremely strong or their setting-up was not worth the effort!

A race at Brands Hatch saw Bruce come up against Ken Tyrrell who was then better known as a lumber merchant in

Surrey. Ken was driving a Formula 2 Cooper for Alan Brown and he took Bruce as they were going into Paddock Bend just after the start. 'I didn't even know him and I was perturbed that he should be going so much faster than I was,' Bruce reported in his book. 'I pulled up beside him at Clearways and he left me standing. I later found he was using second and third gears and high revs, while I had been using third and fourth.' Bruce got past Ken a couple of laps later and went on to win the race.

Tyrrell's version of the race is interesting. 'Bruce had gone very well in practice and everyone was wondering who this new boy was. We knew he had won the award in New Zealand but that was about all. He really looked like a youngster then. I got a better start than he did and got out in front with him close behind. I remember thinking that he was going to have difficulty getting by, but then I imagined the commentator saying, "Why doesn't that old so-and-so Tyrrell get out of the way and let this youngster get on with it." So I moved over and let him by.'

Ten years later Tyrrell was entering a Formula 1 car for Jackie Stewart and a year afterwards he had won the World Championship in a Tyrrell-entered Matra-Ford. Tyrrell's ability as a talent-spotter and team manager have become something of a legend since those early days. In 1959 he signed Bruce to drive one of a pair of Formula 2 Coopers that he was entering together with Alan Brown. 'I thought Bruce would become World Champion because he had the ability to think about it. He wasn't going to be the world's quickest driver, but then the world's quickest driver isn't always World Champion.'

Bruce ran his own Formula 2 car in several more races in England and in Europe, but the race he had set his heart on running was the German Grand Prix which combined Formula 2 and Formula 1 cars to make a full field on the 14.2 mile Nurburgring. Bruce's entry had been placed as first reserve since the German organizers were probably not exactly sure who he was, but John Cooper assured him that someone was bound to crash during practice so that his place at the head of the reserve list was as good as a guaranteed start.

He borrowed passenger cars to try and form the horrors of the 'Ring' into some sort of order and he eventually wound up with a place on the fourth row of the grid behind the 2½-litre BRMs of Harry Schell and Jean Behra. Schell was known as one of the best exponents of the art of anticipating the starter so John Cooper warned Bruce to watch Schell's rear wheels and ignore the flag. He was fifth into the first corner with only four Formula 1 cars ahead of him. John Cooper obviously knew the score too.

By the third lap Bruce was second in the Formula 2 section behind Phil Hill's Ferrari and ahead of Barth's Porsche. When the Ferrari started to run out of brakes, Bruce caught and passed it and held his lead to the finish. He went up on the victory dais and was proudly garlanded alongside Tony Brooks who had won the Grand Prix in a Vanwall. As well as winning the Formula 2 section Bruce had finished fifth overall behind Brooks, the Coopers of Salvadori and Trintignant, and von Tripps in a 2½-litre Ferrari.

The 1958 German Grand Prix, more than any other race that season, made Bruce's name and assured him of a Cooper drive the following season. His effort received the sort of press that Jacky Ickx's race in a Formula 2 Matra at the 'Ring' earned ten years later.

Although he might not have been aware of it at the time in the bustle to get back to England for a race at Brands Hatch the following day, he was on the threshold of a distinguished career as a Grand Prix driver and a racing car designer and builder.

At Brands Hatch a weary McLaren must have been mildly astonished to realize that the commentator, John Bolster, was leading the crowd in singing 'Happy Birthday' as they drove around on the parade lap before the race.

It was August 30, 1958, and Bruce McLaren was twenty-one years old.

2 Driving the Grand Prix Coopers

'I had been shooting at the 1959 European championships in North Wales and I'd gone across to see the British Grand Prix at Aintree. Reg Tanner, competition manager of Esso, was one of the people I had met while brother Jimmy was racing, and I was talking with him in the paddock when this young guy with a limp walked over to the Cooper transporter. Reg said "That's Bruce McLaren, he's got a great future in racing". I remember seeing him then and thinking "Jesus – he's only twenty-one years of age and he's over here from New Zealand and he's driving a Formula 1 works Cooper...."' The speaker was the nineteen-year-old Jackie Stewart, one of the best clay pigeon shooters in Europe, who in five years was to switch to racing cars. Ten years later he won the British Grand Prix himself and the World championship in the same season.

Bruce gave Stewart good value at Aintree. Brabham was out in front in the $2\frac{1}{2}$-litre works Cooper and when Stirling Moss made a couple of pit stops in the apple green front-engined BRM Bruce found himself up in second place just ahead of Moss. The pressure was really on and Bruce was throwing the Cooper all over the place in his efforts to stay ahead of the BRM. Caution and perhaps a tinge of embarrassment prompted him to relinquish his hairily-held place to Stirling, but that didn't mean he had given up. The pair of them traded records in the closing laps and as they took the flag the BRM was just a nose in front of the dark green Cooper. McLaren and Moss shared a new lap record for the 3-mile track at 93.31mph.

At the end of the 1958 season Bruce had fitted a special 1,960cc version of the Formula 2 1.5 litre Coventry Climax engine in his Formula 2 Cooper and shipped it home to New

Zealand. He won at Waimate and Teretonga and collected enough points to clinch the national championships since he was still technically a New Zealand 'local' driver. His factory drive with Cooper later in the year automatically made him an 'overseas' driver for subsequent races at home.

Bruce had been promised a Formula 2 drive with the Cooper team but when he arrived back in England early in 1959 he discovered that different plans had been made over the winter and the Formula 2 team was now being handed over to Ken Tyrrell and Alan Brown who were entering a pair of works-supported cars. Bruce was asked if he would mind driving in the Grand Prix team with Brabham and Masten Gregory and on his instant acceptance he was taken out into the workshops and shown Jack's new 2.5 litre car and the pair of 2.2 litre cars that had been prepared for Bruce and Masten Gregory. By Monaco all three cars were fitted with the full 2.5 litre Climax engines. Any spare weekends Bruce might have had were now taken up with an offer from Ken Tyrrell to drive one of his Formula 2 cars.

At one stage just before the German Grand Prix in 1958 John Cooper, Jack Brabham, Ian Burgess, and the team secretary Andrew Ferguson had a heart-to-heart talk with Bruce to try and make him change his mind about giving it all away and going home to his engineering studies. Now he was very pleased he had decided to stay.

'Pop' and Mrs McLaren had decided to come over to Europe to see their son now that he was a fully-fledged Grand Prix driver, but they were appalled when they witnessed the French Grand Prix at Rheims. A blazingly hot sun melted the road surface and 'cooked' the drivers in the cockpits. Flying stones smashed screens and goggles and slashed the drivers' faces. Bruce staggered exhausted from his battered car and collapsed for the thirty minutes break between the Grand Prix and the Formula 2 race. When he started in the Formula 2 race he was on top of the world, literally 'high' on physical exhaustion, but he realized after a few close shaves that he was scarcely responsible for some of the things he was doing on the high-speed road circuit and he pulled in to retire as Brabham had done a few laps earlier. Bruce's parents were shattered – racing certainly wasn't like this at Ardmore!

Following his dice to third place alongside Moss in the British Grand Prix, Bruce failed to finish a race until the 'circus' crossed the Atlantic for the first American Grand Prix to be held since 1916. It was taking the place of the Moroccan Grand Prix on the championship calendar.

In 1916 the 'Grand Prize' was held on an 8.4 mile road circuit at Santa Monica, California, and it had been won by Johnny Aitken in a 300 cu. in. Peugeot. His own Peugeot had broken a piston on the first lap so he took over Howard Wilcox's car and they shared the victory. The rich American Automobile Association championship hinged on the result of this race. Dario Resta was leading but Aitken could pip him on points in this final event. Resta lost the lead on the 19th lap of the 48-lap race with ignition trouble in his Peugeot and after Aitken had taken over Wilcox's leading car, Resta first protested unsuccessfully and then tried to buy Earl Cooper's Stutz which was then running second! Honour was satisfied when the race went to Aitken and the championship to Resta.

The 1959 American Grand Prix at Sebring was no less exciting, for once again it was to be the decider of the championship, this time the World championship for drivers. The title was being fought out between Brabham with 31 points, Moss with 25½, and Tony Brooks (Ferrari) with 23. If Jack won the race the title was his, but if Stirling beat Jack and took fastest lap, then Moss would be Champion. Brooks had to win and take fastest lap with neither Brabham nor Moss finishing. When the race started Moss took off in the lead with his Walker Cooper ahead of Brabham and McLaren, but when Moss's transmission failed it looked as though the race and the title was being handed on a plate to Brabham. But two laps from the end Jack ran out of petrol! At the last minute he had altered the size of the choke-tubes in his Webers making the engine run richer and with the added effort of towing Bruce round his fuel mileage had dropped drastically. Bruce steered round the slowing Cooper, looking across at Jack and not knowing what he was supposed to do next. If he won, would Jack still be Champion? Should he wait for Jack? He knew instantly that he had no option but to race for the flag because Trintignant's Cooper was only seconds behind him and catching up fast. He won the Grand Prix and revelled in the surprise and glory of it all. At 22 he was the youngest driver ever to win a Grande Epreuve. He was famous.

He might have been famous but he did not really feel very famous. He was still working hard to make a success of his career and he displayed none of the trappings of a famous racing driver. He drove a Morris Minor that he had bought from Betty Brabham, and he shared a little bed-sittingroom in Surbiton with Phil Kerr. This modest apartment boasted one main room that had two beds, a couple of chairs, a wardrobe, and a gas fire. There was a tiny kitchen with an equally tiny gas cooker. The bathroom was on the landing to be shared with the other tenants. Their daily menu included cornflakes and coffee for breakfast, lunch depended on where they were and whether they could afford it, and the evening meal was always at Nick's Café in Kingston down by the coal yards beside the Thames. Their standard order was sausages, bacon and baked beans for one and ninepence. They made themselves instant coffee when they got back to the bedsitter. By comparison Bob Cratchett had it made. On occasions they would be invited out to meals and the high point of the week, when they were home, was a Sunday roast with the Brabham household.

If his way of life was modest away from the tracks the simple fact that he was now a fully-fledged Grand Prix driver and committed to follow the 'circus' around the international calendar gave him a touch of glamour, but he never flaunted it. It probably never occurred to him that living out of a suitcase was glamorous. In 1960 he would race in Argentina, Monaco, Holland, Belgium, Britain, Portugal, Italy and America. His diary logged all these dates interspersed with Formula 2 races and the occasional sports car drive on his 'free' weekends. It was really the beginning of the period when Bruce could only call Wednesday a reasonably safe day to make a dinner date in England. Thursday was spent travelling to the track, Friday and Saturday were practice days, Sunday was race day, and Monday was spent getting home again. Sometimes Tuesday too. So Wednesday was usually the only safe day to guarantee being at home. Or at least in England.

Bruce went back to New Zealand for Christmas and took a 2.5 litre Formula 1 Cooper with him. He finished a couple of seconds behind Brabham's Cooper in the New Zealand Grand Prix at Ardmore and while the evening's sporting papers wondered whether Bruce had driven to team orders and let Jack win, Bruce was proposing to Patty. Three months later Patty flew to England to tour the races with her new fiancé and to act as his secretary. This time Bruce had to cut short the New Zealand races and fly to South America for the Argentinian Grand Prix in February. Shipping delays meant that Jack and Bruce had scarcely any practice on the Buenos Aires track and when the race started the two BRMs, the new rear-engined Lotus and Moss's Cooper were out in front of the works Coopers. The temperature was well over 100° in the shade and Bruce had taken the precaution of fitting a flask of iced orange juice in his cockpit, having learned his lesson after the roasting at Rheims the season before. Innes Ireland led in the new Lotus but spun on the second lap, dropping to sixth and then fighting back to second place only to break a steering arm bolt when he clobbered a kerb and dropped back to a slowing sixth. The BRMs had valve spring problems, Moss broke a suspension arm after hitting a kerb, and Brabham's gearbox failed. Bruce was on his own out in front for the second Grand Prix in succession and he opened up a 26.3sec lead on Cliff Allison's Ferrari to win at an average of 84.6mph.

The new rear-engined Lotus called for a crash programme to design a new Cooper to defend their World title and the new low-line was designed, built and tested in two months. Owen

'The Beard' Maddocks had spent the winter designing a completely new five-speed gearbox to counter the endless problems they had found with the Citroen-based transmission the season before, so Bruce summoned up his knowledge of technical drawings to assist in the design office, laying out wishbone assemblies and other components to hasten the progress of the new car. This progress was hindered somewhat by Charles Cooper, John's father, insisting that the new car had to be designed to allow for the old Cooper rear leaf spring to be replaced if the new coil springs proved to be unsuitable. After the first day of testing the prototype at Silverstone Brabham lowered the lap record by six seconds, and the old leaf spring ideas were conveniently forgotten.

Rain in the race at Monaco turned the street circuit into a skating rink and Moss gave Lotus their first Grand Prix win, with Bruce in second place. As they moved on to Zandvoort, McLaren was leading the Championship, a point which was not lost on the Dutch organizers who had refused the 'unknown' driver an entry the previous year. A driveshaft failure dropped Bruce from the race. Brabham won at Zandvoort and during the season he was to win again at Spa, Silverstone, and Oporto to take his second World Championship. Bruce was second to Jack at Spa and Oporto and adding these points to his score from winning the Argentina Grand Prix and finishing second at Monaco, he was second in the Championship with 37 points behind Jack on 43, and ahead of Moss with 19. Stirling missed two races that season after crashing at Spa and breaking both legs.

The 1960 season was the last under the 2.5 litre formula and it was the last of the so-called Golden Years for the Cooper team. All the British cars, with the exception of the Walker Lotus driven by Moss, were to be outpaced by the superior power of the V6 Ferraris which had been developed as Formula 2 cars the year before. The British constructors tended to regard the formula change as something horrible which might go away if they shut their eyes and ignored it, and this attitude was to cost them dearly during 1961.

Brabham decided he could do things better his way at the end of the season and left the Cooper team to build his own cars and this resulted in a touchy period at the Cooper factory because Charles Cooper maintained that Jack had taken all the team's secrets with him when he left and Bruce was effectively barred from the drawing office. This was hardly a way to encourage developments and Cooper fortunes sagged as other constructors overtook their rear-engined lead. Ferrari won the manufacturers' championship in 1961, BRM in 1962, Lotus in 1963, Ferrari again in 1964, Lotus again in 1965, and in 1966 Brabham won the Championship for constructors and drivers in his own car.

Patty had stayed in England over the winter of 1960–1 working as a beautician while Bruce went home to a mediocre series of races in New Zealand with a 2½-litre Cooper. Back in England Phil Kerr had bought an apartment which allowed them the luxury of a bedroom each, a lounge, a bathroom that they did not have to share with everyone else in the building and a kitchen big enough so that you did not have to go outside to turn round. Phil remembers these bachelor days well. 'Bruce never became domesticated and never showed any likelihood of becoming that way. Housework was beyond him and although we were supposed to be taking it in turns to keep the flat tidy, I always seemed to have to do it. On a weekend when Bruce would be away racing, I would get the place all sorted out spick and span, but within five minutes of Bruce's return the whole place would be a shambles. He would walk in the front door and there would be a trail of clothes and suitcases and shoes and packages of things he'd bought while he was away. This trail would go across the lounge and into his bedroom where he would open his suitcase and then there would be a trail of clothes from his bedroom to the bathroom. It was turmoil and yet he always seemed to be quite oblivious to it all . . .'

One story surrounded one of Bruce's rare forays to the launderette with a bag of washing which included his favourite short-sleeved blue sports shirt that he always wore when driving. It had become almost a mascot. As far as Bruce was concerned, the laundry machine was foolproof providing you remembered to put in the washing, the soap powder and the sixpence. It wasn't until he got back to the flat and started to empty out the laundry bag that he realized all the white underpants, vests, shirts and sweaters were a delicate shade of light blue.

'When he saw what had happened, he just couldn't stop laughing. He sat down and laughed until the tears were rolling down his cheeks and his sides ached. He just hooted and rolled about until he couldn't bear it. That's what life tended to be like in the flat.'

The Morris Minor had been sold to make way for a splendid 3.8 Jaguar which Bruce had bought with the intention of shipping it home for his father. 'I bought it new from the factory with high compression, a high ratio rear axle, racing suspension, and high-geared steering,' Bruce wrote for a feature on road cars he had owned. 'The high-geared steering was the one mistake I made with the 3.8. It was just too heavy to be pleasant on the road and it made the car "darty" but it was great fun if you wanted to do a couple of laps round Goodwood between testing sessions. It was one of the most reliable cars I've ever owned in direct contrast to the E Type that came next. It was one of the first Es and when it was brand new it was a positive joy, but I made the mistake of fitting a rear end that was too high. I opted for the 2.9 Le Mans axle ratio because I figured that with this sort of car you could cruise quite happily at 120mph, but when I tried doing that across Europe I found that I didn't really want to go that fast after all.'

At the end of the 1961 season Bruce and Patty flew back to New Zealand and they were married in November in Christchurch. They had a brief honeymoon in Fiji and returned to run the series of races in New Zealand and Australia with a special 2.7 litre low-line Cooper that Bruce had bought from Tommy Atkins and he had hired Tommy's chief mechanic, Harry Pearce, to look after the car. He had a series of races to minor places with a jet dash back to England in between to check progress on the new Formula 1 car for 1962.

In Melbourne after he had finished third behind Brabham and Surtees in their Coopers, Bruce offered me a job as his secretary back in England. He said he was not sure quite what I would do, but he would think of something. He had been under the impression that I was going back to England anyway, but when I told him I had a job lined up with a newspaper in Hobart, Tasmania, he offered to advance me the cost of the air fare against my first year's wages. I accepted his offer and flew back to England via Sebring with Bruce and Patty and worked during 1962 for £6 per week sharing a small flat with Wally Willmott, a mechanic from my hometown who was to become Bruce's first permanent mechanic.

The new Cooper with the Climax V8 engine and new six-speed gearbox arrived just in time for the Dutch Grand Prix at Zandvoort which opened the Championship in 1962, but the plaudits of the press were strictly reserved for the new monocoque Lotus 25. Stirling Moss had been lucky to escape with his life when his Lotus 24 crashed at Goodwood in the Easter Monday meeting and this new Lotus with Jim Clark at the wheel was to be the dominant combination of the decade.

Bruce won the Monaco Grand Prix after Clark's Lotus and Hill's BRM had failed and he won the non-championship Formula 1 race at Rheims but it was six years before Bruce was to win another Formula 1 race – and then it was to be in his own car.

After a second place in the South Africa Grand Prix that ended the 1962 season, Bruce was placed third in the World championship with 27 points behind Graham Hill in the BRM who won the title with 42 points, and Jimmy Clark in the new Lotus with 30 points.

The 1963 season was notable mainly for a series of accidents. Patty set the ball rolling when a water ski-ing boat capsized in Australia and she was hit by the propeller as she was swimming away. The bones in her left ankle and heel were badly smashed and she spent weeks in plaster and months in pain. Before the season had started in Europe, John Cooper crashed in a mysterious accident with an experimental twin-engined Mini on the Kingston-By-Pass, and Ken Tyrrell stepped in to assist Charles Cooper in looking after the Formula 1 team. Bruce rounded off the trio of accidents when his Cooper went end-over-end at the Nurburgring and he was rushed unconscious to the hospital on the hillside behind the little village of Adenau. When he came to he had two very sore legs, a black eye and absolutely no recollection about what had happened. Back in England he hobbled into the workshops and winced when he saw the twisted broken pile of junk that had been his racing car. Piecing together the bits, they came to the conclusion that the right rear wishbone had broken.

Bruce was tempering his growing frustration with the lack of development at Coopers and his own lack of success. People were beginning to comment on the dimming of the McLaren star, and there were those who blamed Bruce for the Cooper lack of success. This was a particularly difficult time for him. He felt that he knew what had to be done, but it was becoming increasingly difficult for him to have his suggestions acted upon. There was a new formula for the 1964 series of races in New Zealand and Australia which limited engine capacity to $2\frac{1}{2}$-litres and race distances were to be pegged at 100 miles. Bruce wanted to build a pair of special Coopers and enter them as works cars on the new-style Tasman series, but Charles Cooper blocked each approach that Bruce made. McLaren's idea was to build a pair of slimline lightweight cars to take advantage of the regulations, but Charles argued that a regular Formula 1 car fitted with a $2\frac{1}{2}$-litre engine could do the job. There was also a problem of entries for Timmy Mayer as a 'works' driver because Down Under he was unknown, and Charles said that if there was to be any doubt about the validity of the entries he would cancel the whole operation.

At this stage Bruce decided to do it on his own and after discussions with Teddy Mayer, Tim's brother, they agreed to share costs and run under Bruce's own colours. Necessity bred Bruce McLaren Motor Racing Limited, and the racing artist

Michael Turner designed a team badge with a kiwi as the main motif. The Coopers became more McLarens as the build programme progressed. The bulky side-tanks of the Formula 1 Coopers were not needed on the short Tasman races, so the tubular spaceframe was wrapped in steel sheet which helped to stiffen the chassis and acted as the body sides. The fuel was carried in a seat tank and a couple of smaller top tanks. The Cooper top rear wishbone was replaced with a top link and radius arm and the McLaren-Cooper was ready to race.

Brabham had also built a pair of special cars for the Series so it was a full-scale battle between the McLaren and Brabham camps. Denny Hulme won Levin for Brabham, but Bruce won the New Zealand Grand Prix on the new Pukekohe track outside Auckland and Timmy was third behind Denny's Brabham. Bruce had been trying for eight years to win his hometown Grand Prix and at last he had succeeded. He followed this with wins at Wigram and Teretonga after torrid battles with the Brabhams.

Luck left the little team in Australia. Jack won at Warwick Farm with Bruce second and Timmy third. At Lakeside Timmy was starting to display the sort of polished prowess that had prompted Ken Tyrrell to sign him for Formula Junior and later a place in the Cooper Grand Prix team for the coming season. He led the race until his engine blew up, and Bruce finished third behind Tasmanian John Youl's Cooper and Denny's Brabham. In practice for the final race of the Series at Longford in Tasmania, a fast $4\frac{1}{2}$-mile track over public roads strongly reminiscent of Rheims, Timmy's Cooper became airborne over a bump just before the braking area and smashed into a track-side tree. Timmy was killed instantly. On race day Bruce started sorrowfully from the back of the grid in no mood to go racing for the Tasman title, but he finished second to Hill's Brabham and won the Tasman championship.

The die was cast. He had proved to himself that he knew enough about racing now to build his own cars and run his own racing team. Racing was beginning to get exciting again. The old challenge had returned. In *From the Cockpit* he outlined his mounting enjoyment as his Tasman Coopers took shape for the 1964 Series. 'The first essential for success in racing is enthusiasm. Not just mild, but burning enthusiasm. To succeed in motor racing or in any sport it must be the most important thing in your life.

'This goes for many things other than motor racing in particular or sport in general, because if it isn't the most important thing to you, there are a dozen other people to whom it is. Those are the people you have to beat.

'You must eat, live and think motor racing. The more you think about it and plan, the better you will do. "Scheme" is probably a better word than "think". Stirling Moss used to think about motor racing more than anyone else I know and John Surtees comes a close second. Jack Brabham is another for whom his sport is everything.

'When I get wound up in a project, whether it is one of Cooper's new Formula 1 cars or building my own cars for New Zealand and Australia, everything else is made secondary to it. Everything. I often force myself to go to sleep when trying to worry out a problem, or I am stuck with it all night. I decided long ago that solid sleep is one of the first essentials when trying to work hard. It is more a question of attitude of mind than anything else. The people who succeed in racing are those who would do so in any walk of life.

'First comes natural ability – and there are hundreds with it – but there must always be the dedication to want to apply it, continue applying it and keep improving it.

'Motor racing is unlike some other sports, in fact it is sometimes argued that it isn't a sport at all because one uses machinery and its efficiency is the important thing. This is true, of course, but it is common knowledge that with any good piece of equipment, be it a good gun, a good yacht, or a good racing car, one person or one crew will do better with it than others – and here lies the big difference between one competitor and the next.

'I like to feel that the combination of driver and car is

important. I'm sure Jack Brabham feels the same way and that's why he is building his own car. By winning with one's own car, both other drivers and other cars have been beaten.

'The usual ambition once a person becomes serious about motor racing is to be a works driver. This is the pinnacle of GP racing, but one can go beyond it, full circle. The normal beginning is driving one's own car . . . when driving my own Formula 2 car in 1958, my big ambition was to become a works driver for the Cooper factory. Now I enjoy nothing better than running my own cars again.'

3 *The First McLaren Cars*

If any one man were to blame for the McLaren involvement in American sports car racing, it would have to be Briggs Cunningham, the wealthy sportsman and sports car lover who tried for years to win Le Mans with his own Cunningham cars. His first effort was in 1950 with a Cadillac saloon and a Cunningham sports car that looked as though it had been styled by the designer of the WW1 tank. The French called it 'Le Monstre'. The saloon was tenth that year and the monster was eleventh. The following year he returned with new Chrysler-engined C2R Cunninghams and one was lying a safe second behind the Walker-Whitehead C Type Jaguar with four hours to go when engine and transmission trouble dropped it to an eventual eighteenth place. In 1952 Briggs himself drove a C4R into fourth place after being at the wheel for twenty of the twenty-four hours. In 1953 a C5R Cunningham was third and was the fastest car down the Mulsanne straight at 154.8mph. A C4R was third in 1954.

Briggs bought racing cars like other people shop in supermarkets. He had to have one of everything on the shelf. In 1960 Bruce was invited to drive the prototype development of the Jaguar D Type that was eventually to become the production E Type, at Laguna Seca. It was his first sports car race in America and he finished fifth which came as something of a surprise to the Cunningham crew who frankly had not expected the car even to qualify on the tight Monterey circuit. The next day, on the flight back to New York, Bruce met Roger Penske. Briggs ordered a copy of the 1961 works Formula 1 Cooper to be painted in the American racing colours and delivered to the American Grand Prix at Watkins Glen for Walt Hansgen to drive, but unfortunately Walt wrecked the car. Penske entered the saga again by buying the wrecked Cooper and having it rebuilt for Formula Libre racing. Teddy Mayer rented the Cooper for brother Timmy to race and Tyler Alexander looked after it.

At Sebring in 1961 Briggs asked Bruce to drive for him again sharing a rear-engined V12 Type 63 Birdcage Maserati with Hansgen but it failed in the race with engine and transmission problems. Bruce would have driven this car again at Le Mans that year, if Walt had not parked it in a sandbank in the early stages of the race.

The Cunningham entry at Sebring in 1962 was a special Cooper Monaco fitted with a 2.8 litre 4-cylinder Maserati engine and Bruce drove it with Roger Penske. The car led early in the race until it was slowed with electrical problems. At that race Roger talked with Bruce about his plans for fitting a sports car body on his Formula Libre Cooper to contest the professional races at Laguna Seca and Riverside at the end of the season. Roger even asked Bruce if he would join him in the venture, but Bruce had his own plans. Roger had permission from the race organizers to build his sports car as a centre-seater and with what was essentially a Grand Prix car with a 2.7 litre Climax engine, he had a 200-lb. weight advantage on the works Coopers and he won both the big-money races in California that season. The car had been christened the Zerex Special for commercial reasons.

The people he beat, including Bruce in the works Cooper Monaco, argued later that the car was hardly within international regulations governing sports car racing (shades of the 2J Chaparral in 1970!) and for 1963 Roger had to alter the Zerex by cutting a slice out each side of the tube frame and inserting curved piping to make room for two seats, thus complying with the rules.

As Bruce mentioned later, a master plumber would have been delighted with the tube bends but they gave the chassis one of the lowest torsional rigidity figures ever. Roger won the Guards

Trophy at Brands Hatch with the 'legalized' Zerex and then sold the car to John Mecom and drove for the Mecom team.

Sports cars using big American V8s had started to become competitive and the 'little' 2.7 litre Zerex with its Climax engine was parked and almost forgotten under a dust cover in the corner of Mecom's big workshops. A 3.5 litre aluminium F85 Oldsmobile V8 engine sat in a crate beside the Zerex waiting for an engine swap when someone had the time.

So in a roundabout sort of way it was Briggs Cunningham who brought Bruce into American sports car racing, it was Briggs who bought the original Cooper that was to become the Zerex, and Briggs who brought Roger and Bruce together when the Zerex was about to take shape in the first place.

Bruce had entertained ideas of building a Zerex type of sports car before he went out to New Zealand at the end of 1963 since this would enable him to use his supply of Climax engines which he could otherwise use only on the Australasian races. In fact he had built a prototype tubular chassis. At that stage the fiercely defended McLaren pet theory was that a good lightweight reliable car with a Climax engine was still the equal of all-comers, but Tyler and Wally had been to Nassau and seen just how competitive the big American-engined sports cars were becoming and they were not at all keen to support Bruce.

They finally settled on a compromise, buying the Zerex with the spare Oldsmobile engine, and the car arrived in England with Tyler just three days before the Oulton Park race in April. Wally and Tyler sweated to fit the regulation luggage trunk and spare wheel in time for the race, but after all their work the car retired with no oil pressure. At Aintree and Silverstone it was a different story and Bruce beat Jim Clark in the Lotus 30 and Roy Salvadori in a Monaco fitted with a 5-litre Maserati engine.

The day after their win at Silverstone the Zerex was stripped and chopped up. The entire section of the frame from just behind the front suspension to just ahead of the rear suspension was scrapped and a new McLaren-designed tube frame was welded in. This was far stiffer than the willowy Zerex chassis and it had the sophistication of the water and oil flowing through the chassis tubes. Bruce left Wally and Tyler with a wire model of the chassis and went down to Monaco where the new Cooper with inboard front suspension broke a front upright in practice and Bruce wrecked it. He drove a 1963 Cooper in the race and retired early with an oil leak. From there he went to the Nurburgring to drive the new GT40 Ford in its first race with Phil Hill. They were second fastest in practice and lying second in the race to the works Ferrari at one stage but they were eliminated when the suspension broke.

Back in England the new chassis had been completed and the Oldsmobile engine had been installed. Due to time, space and suspension geometry they had decided to use the 'old faithful' Colotti Type 21 five-speed transmission from Bruce's Tasman Cooper. There was no time to fabricate a proper exhaust system so the car was flown to Canada for the Mosport race with eight stub exhausts poking up through the tail.

The car had three names in all. The chassis had been completed on a Sunday morning, so Bruce decided that it should be painted there and then. The fact that there was no paint available and no hardware shops likely to be open on the Sabbath was of little consequence. I was despatched to find a tin of paint and I eventually returned with a tin of garden gate green unearthed in a handyman's shop that was just on the point of closing. The colour was appalling, but it was paint and when we had finished the frame gleamed bright green. It cried out to be called the Jolly Green Giant. It was also the Zerex Special re-framed and re-engined, but for various reasons Bruce decreed that it should be officially known as the Cooper-Oldsmobile. He was involving himself in a very political situation because he was still number one driver in the Cooper team and yet he was actively engaged in building a sports car that was to beat the factory-built Cooper Monacos. Charles and John Cooper could not help but be reminded of Jack's project to build a Formula Junior car which had preceded his leaving the team and it must have seemed obvious that Bruce was about to do exactly the same. To have called the revised car a McLaren would have meant immediate ructions within the Cooper team and Bruce was most reluctant to upset his relationship and jeopardize his Formula 1 drive. The idea of a McLaren Formula 1 car was then only a remote possibility on the horizon for the little team, and Bruce was also aware that an alternative Formula 1 seat might be rather difficult to find. So officially the car was a Cooper-Oldsmobile when Bruce won with it at Mosport in June.

Bruce drove the Cooper-Olds to another win in the Guards Trophy at Brands Hatch at the end of August, but between Mosport and Brands he had been working hard transferring the team from the incredibly slum-like conditions in the tractor shed at New Malden to what I had hopefully described in a press release as 'a spotless new 3,000 sq. ft. racing workshop'. Looking back now, the premises in Belvedere Works behind the new shopping complex that was just being built at Feltham, were only slightly less slumlike than the tractor shed. But a thorough clean-out and a carpentry job saw offices for management (Bruce, Teddy and myself) and design staff (Eddie Stait and later Robin Herd), a workshop area where the Tasman Coopers and the sports cars were prepared, and a prototype shop closed off at the end where the GTX Ford was to be built.

While Bruce was winning the Guards Trophy an all-new sports car was nearing completion. It was a spaceframe development of the Cooper-Oldsmobile, but it used stressed magnesium sheet in the cockpit area to strengthen the frame. The side members were set low to clear the exhaust system of the Oldsmobile which was being built by Traco Engineering in Los Angeles. It was now out to 3.9 litres and giving 340 horsepower. The F85 engine was the ill-fated early attempt by General Motors to use aluminium instead of cast iron for the cylinder blocks, but complications in the casting processes proved costly and the idea was scrapped. Teddy Mayer was offering good prices for F85 engines from scrap yards and Traco were re-working them into racing shape.

The new McLaren used Cooper wheels, uprights and steering arms, and a Hewland gearbox. Fitted with the 3.9 litre engine from the Zerex, the McLaren M1 lowered the Zerex's record at Goodwood by a clear three seconds.

The car was painted black with a silver stripe (New Zealand's sporting colours) and it was the fastest car on the track at Mosport in September but a throttle linkage broke and after a long pit stop Bruce came out again to hammer the lap record and finish third. In England Frank Nichols of Elva Cars had called at the Feltham factory suggesting an association between McLaren and Elva to build production versions of the sports car for sale, and a deal was eventually worked out with Peter Agg and John Bennett of Trojan, Elva's parent company, to build McLaren replicas. They were to be called McLaren-Elvas.

At Riverside Bruce qualified the black car second to Gurney's Lotus 19 and blasted off into a lead that in three laps had put him nine seconds clear of the field. Then a water hose blew off. He lost four minutes in the pits and then climbed back up to third place when the hose blew off again. At Laguna Seca another water hose blew off. Before Nassau the car was painted an orangy red colour in place of the sombre black, and Bruce finished second to Penske in Hap Sharp's Chaparral.

It became apparent to Bruce that it was much more difficult winning once he had put his own name on the nose than it had been when he was driving the Cooper-Olds. Jack Brabham had also discovered that it was an uphill slog once your own name was on your racing car. But for both men, their perseverance was to pay off.

Bruce's Formula 1 record in 1964 was scarcely worthy of notice, his best finishes being seconds at Spa and Monza. Looking back over Bruce's record he seemed to do well at these fast tracks. At Monza he was third in 1961, 1962 and 1963 and in 1964 he was second. At Spa he was second in 1960, 1963, and 1964, he was third in 1965, and in 1968 he won the race in his own car.

Bruce took a pair of Coopers home to defend his Tasman

title in January and February of 1965 with Phil Hill as number two in the Cooper Bruce had used the previous season. A new car based on the 1964 Formula 1 Cooper with inboard front suspension had been built for Bruce with the engine bay altered to take the 4-cylinder FPF Climax engine in place of the Climax V8. Both cars had Hewland gearboxes and both were set-up to take 13-inch wheels on Dunlop tyres.

The McLaren contract with Firestone meant a last-minute switch to 15-inch wheels all round since Firestone were making their first appearance in European racing and they only had 15-inch Indianapolis tyres available. Phil's car stayed in England to test tyres and was flown out to New Zealand at a cost of £1,880 just in time for the New Zealand Grand Prix. The new tyres made both cars almost unmanageable, and it was not until the final race of the series – the Australian Grand Prix at Longford – that Bruce managed to come up with a winning combination. It was Firestone's first Grand Prix win.

Chris Amon was signed on as second driver with the McLaren team in 1965 to run tyre tests for Firestone with the original McLaren sports car, and he was also to get drives in the American races. Bruce always maintained that Chris had an enormous amount of natural talent if only he could be taken in hand and disciplined. He had learned about racing with a 250F Maserati when he was seventeen, and Reg Parnell had brought him into Grand Prix racing in Europe two years later but at the end of his first season overseas Reg had died. Since then Chris had been roaming around in the racing wilderness 'going to seed'. With Bruce in 1965 Chris learned about test driving and tyre development and was later to become one of Firestone's best test men.

Chris drove the original M1A sports car to win at St Jovite early in 1965 while Bruce was racing to fifth place at Monaco in the Cooper Formula 1 car, and when Bruce burned his neck when the engine caught alight during practice for the Martini Trophy at Silverstone, Chris took his place, started from the back of the grid and won the race.

Silverstone was the venue for the epic dice between Surtees in the Lola T70 and Bruce in the M1A that resulted in the narrowest of wins for Bruce. He was running new rear rims that were twelve inches across and he reckoned these to be nearing the ultimate in rubber rollers. But five years later the McLarens had 20-inch rear rims. . . .

Bruce led both heats of the Mosport sports car race the day after Indianapolis that year but he retired both times with a broken transmission. Tyler had changed gearboxes between heats, but the same thing happened again, so Tyler trailed the car to his home in Boston and altered the car to take the German ZF transmission in place of the Hewland. A few days later Bruce had a hectic dice with Jim Hall's Chaparral at Ste Jovite and won.

Back in England the designers were already working on the M1B, a sports car that was to have a new and more efficient shape evolved by Michael Turner, the artist, working with Tyler and Robin Herd. It had a blunter nose and a sharper cut-off on the tail. Tyler applied all the techniques he had learned in aircraft building to the ducting inside the nose of the new car making a proper integral structure that formed the ducts and also held the radiator. To strengthen the space-frame (the M1A had been nicknamed FlexiPower) Herd mounted a production chassis straight from Trojan to the most substantial piece of ironmongery in the workshop – the steel cutting guillotine – and with a piece of channel section wrought iron he made an enormous cantilever hanging weights on it to take deflection measurements, adding tubes or cutting them out until he had a chassis that was twenty per cent stronger than the M1A and was no heavier.

The first race for the M1B at Ste Jovite resulted in oily and ignominious retirement in practice when the Oldsmobile blew up in a most comprehensive manner, wrecking the transmission as well. Before Mosport a new 4.5 litre engine had arrived from Traco and with this fitted Bruce finished second to Hall's Chaparral. The GTX Ford was ready for this race but it soon became obvious that it was better suited to the long distance endurance races than the shorter sprints.

Phil Hill stood in for Bruce at Kent finishing second in the first heat and was leading the second when he somehow jammed his heel and bent the throttle which meant a pit stop to free it.

Bruce was back at the wheel for Riverside, a race that he dearly wanted to win, and he was fastest in practice but on the start-line he kept putting the car in and out of gear waiting for the starter to make up his mind and when the flag finally dropped Bruce found himself lurching away in third gear by mistake. This botched start fried the clutch and after twelve laps he pitted with a puncture. He hurtled back into the race in one of his typical McLaren hell-bent pursuits of the lead a full lap and 20sec behind leader Hap Sharp's Chaparral. Suffice it to say that he finished 15sec behind Sharp and right on the exhausts of Jim Clark's Lotus having made up more than a lap!

Chris Amon finished fifth at Riverside in the GTX which by this time had been christened 'Big Ed' after another Ford project that had been less than a complete success.

The 1965 season might have been short on concrete results for Team McLaren, but it was a significant season for developments. The GTX had been completed by Gary Knutson and raced in North America (it was to win the Sebring 12-hour race in 1966), Robin Herd had joined the design staff and a Formula 1 prototype car had been built, plans were being made to move to a larger factory at Colnbrook and Bruce was about to leave the Cooper team after eight years.

Although there had been some uncomfortable situations between the Cooper organization and Bruce's own racing activities, he was very much aware that he had learned everything about racing during his years with the team. He was also aware that he had been given his big chance with Coopers, and he left the team with genuinely mixed feelings.

He wrote in *Autosport*, 'The heat of Grand Prix racing is something like the heat of battle – it either welds people together or breaks them apart. In the eight years I have been with Coopers I have to think very hard to remember a cross word between John and myself. In motor racing that's something of a record – perhaps eight years with a Formula 1 team is something of a record too . . .

'When I started to race with John, I was very young and I blush to think of the stories that he can, and is liable to tell you of those early days when I was very much a green Kiwi. With Coopers I learned a lot about racing cars and racing people, and I spent those formative years from twenty to twenty-six with people like John and the men around him – Brabham, Salvadori, Ken Tyrrell – and Charles Cooper who started the whole story with the car he built for John. It's due in part to the influence, the example and the success of these people that makes it possible for me to attempt Grand Prix racing with my own team.'

His own team that November were like one-armed paper-hangers preparing for Formula 1 and the newly-named CanAm sports car series in 1966 as well as the move to Colnbrook. The office door had a sign on it that read 'DON'T KNOCK – WE DON'T HAVE THAT SORT OF TIME!' and it was almost literally true.

To try out Robin Herd's advanced design ideas in metal, M2A – the prototype Formula 1 car – was completed in September. The monocoque was made of Mallite which was a sort of sandwich with aluminium sheet 'bread' and a filling of balsa wood. It was riveted and glued together and as Robin said later, it was strong enough to transport a tank over rough territory. For those test miles in 1965 the chassis was fitted with a wet-sump, 4.5 litre Oldsmobile V8 which was presumed to provide the amount of power and torque that would be available from a 3-litre engine the following season. This car was used for extensive Firestone testing and was later fitted with the first of the McLaren-built 4-cam Indy Ford engines de-stroked to 3-litres for Formula 1.

The car had been built and tested several times before rumours of its existence leaked out to the press. It was easy to deny the existence of a Formula 1 car since the M2A had a 4½-litre engine and was strictly a tyre-test vehicle – it was also important to deny any ideas of a McLaren Formula 1 car while Bruce was still driving for the Cooper team. The cloak-and-dagger routine on the telephone had its serious side too.

M2B was the pukka 1966 Formula 1 car for Bruce and Chris Amon had been retained to drive a second car later in the season. The expected horsepower of the Ford fell far short of the target figure and with barely 300 horsepower Bruce qualified tenth fastest at Monaco. He made a fantastic start, helped probably by the weight of the engine over the Firestones and in the opening laps he was up to sixth place before an oil union came loose and he pitted with oil pouring everywhere.

Bruce was to suffer yet another year of Formula 1 frustration, working to make his own cars competitive and losing out badly as his engines let him down. The Italian Serenissima 3-litre V8 hastily fitted in time for Spa gave up in practice when the bearings failed, but at Brands Hatch in the British Grand Prix Bruce scored his first point in his own car when he finished sixth. The Ford was worked-over and re-fitted for the United States GP where he finished fifth, but at Mexico the engine failed again. They had gambled on the Ford and failed. Brabham had gambled on the Repco version of the F85 Oldsmobile and won. In spades.

At Le Mans in the middle of the season Bruce and Chris shared the winning 7-litre Ford GT after running a copybook race to team orders. The year before Chris had shared a Ford with Phil Hill and had led out on the opening lap until he was joined by Bruce in another works Ford and they led the race 1–2 during the opening hour. For 1966 the two drivers were in the same car and Ford orders were to take it easy. Chris takes up the story. 'I think they considered Bruce and I were reasonably reliable drivers and not likely to get carried away and race with our own team, so we weren't told much before the start. Bruce and I talked a lot about what we would do in the race. We were fairly certain that Dan Gurney would go fast at the start and if this happened we knew Ken Miles would go after him, so Bruce and I decided to hang back. We knew we couldn't afford to get very far behind, but at the same time we couldn't afford to get involved in a race with our team-mates.

'This is actually what happened in the race, of course. Gurney took off and Miles chased him and at one stage we were a lap behind. But I think this paid off the next morning when both Gurney and Miles had troubles with their brakes – largely because they had gone a lot faster than we had the night before.

'We started off lapping around 3min 35sec whereas Miles and Gurney were lapping at around 3min 33sec. By about 2.00am on Sunday it looked as though the Ferrari challenge had failed and we received strict slowing-down instructions. We found 3min 40sec comfortable, but just after dawn orders came to slow down to four minutes, which was close to half a minute slower than we were capable of lapping and it took me something like ten laps of concentrated effort to slow down to this speed. I found that we could do this by saving about 800 revs on the straight, 800 revs through the gears and barely using the brakes at all. This became very monotonous. When you're going hard the time seems to pass quickly but when you are just cruising round the spells take for ever. We had to stop for fuel every hour and a half but the spells seemed to take five times as long as that.

'Bruce reckoned that he never liked sleeping at Le Mans because he had always been woken in the past by someone telling him the car had broken. I never did get to sleep properly in 1966. The most sleep I had was about three quarters of an hour somewhere around eight o'clock on Sunday morning, but surprisingly I didn't feel tired during the race.

'It was the first time I'd seen the dawn at Le Mans and I must say it was a very pleasant sight to see the sun start to come up and we knew we had the night behind us. But then I looked at my watch and realized that we had another eleven hours to go! The sun came up around six and it looked as though it would be a good day, but later in the morning it clouded over and started to rain. The car had been good when it rained during the night. But in the rain on Sunday afternoon with all the oil and rubber about, the track was extremely slippery. This meant that even going through slow corners in first gear with the throttle right off we were going too fast and we had to put the clutch out going through Mulsanne, Arnage and Tertre Rouge . . .'

They won the race in the hotly disputed photo finish from the Miles/Hulme car, Bruce maintaining that he had driven slowly side by side with Miles on that last half of the last lap but that Miles had been hanging back and Bruce wondered if Ken would jump him on the line. Denny and Chris were being interviewed on television as the two cars came up to the line and suddenly the interviewer found himself alone with his microphone. The excitement had been too much for the drivers and they were running to the finishing line!

Amon's chance of a McLaren Formula 1 drive faded with the horsepower curve of the 4-cam Ford and after showing impressive pace on the CanAm series he signed to drive for Ferrari and was to lead their Grand Prix team for three seasons, before switching to the British March team and then the French Matra team for 1971. Grand Prix wins continued to evade him.

It became obvious early in 1966 that the 5-litre Traco-Oldsmobile engines were going to be no match for the 6-litre iron Chevrolets in the Lolas driven by Hulme and Surtees, and after the opening races in Canada Bruce switched from the aluminium engine to a 5.4 litre cast iron Chevrolet which weighed some 200lb. more than the Oldsmobile but gave 100 extra horsepower. After the first CanAm race in the fall the capacity of both cars was upped to 6-litres, but this didn't bring race wins. Both Bruce and Chris were pace makers but they were not winners. Bruce tried Hilborn fuel injection at Laguna Seca and both cars were so fitted for Riverside but in the heat the injection system gave trouble and for the final race at Las Vegas they were back on carburettors and Bruce finished second to the Series winner, Surtees.

The 1966 season had been the first year for the new Grand Prix formula and it was the first running of the CanAm sports car series. The McLaren team had expected to do well in both fields, but by the end of the season they had little to show for their efforts.

'One would have thought that after a very dispiriting year like that everyone would have been so depressed that they would have wanted to jack it in,' says Robin Herd. 'But the result was completely the opposite. Everyone was ten times more determined to do better the following year. It seems strange that when you are successful it's difficult to be determined but when you're unsuccessful determination comes very easily . . .'

The 1967 season was another lost year in Formula 1 for Bruce. The BRM V12 engine had been promised in time for the first Grand Prix but it never arrived until the Canadian Grand Prix in September. To fill in time Bruce drove one of the pretty little M4 Formula 2 cars in the early Formula 2 races and built up a special Formula 1 version by fitting the 2-litre Tasman BRM V8 in place of the 1,600cc Cosworth-Ford FVA unit. At Monaco Bruce was up to second place with this car when the battery went flat and he finished fourth. At Zandvoort he spun the car into a fence on the first lap, and the car was finally gutted by fire during Goodyear tests at Goodwood. Dan Gurney gave Bruce drives in one of his V12 Eagles in the French, British and German Grands Prix but engine trouble put him out of each race. The M5 monocoque had been waiting in the workshops since the beginning of the year and when the V12 engine arrived Bruce did thirty miles round Goodwood and went straight to Canada. For want of a nail this particular McLaren horse lost the Grand Prix. They had decided to run the car without the alternator to save weight and the battery went flat. The car handled extremely well in the rain despite its lack of testing and Bruce was up to second place behind Denny Hulme until the rain eased and Jim Clark went past into second place again with the Lotus 49. Another rain shower would have meant a McLaren advantage again but the drained battery was causing the V12 to lose its edge and the oil pressure was also starting to sag. Before the race ended Hulme had stopped with a visor to combat the rain and Clark's engine had failed. For want of an alternator . . .

At Monza the McLaren-BRM qualified on the front row of the grid with Clark and Brabham, comfortably faster than the works H16 BRMs. The V12 had been developed purely as a 'customer engine' and was meant as a sports car unit. The McLaren was painted red and during practice the organizers had been pressing the crew to paint the car green in accordance with the International regulations. When they realized that the McLaren was the only red car on the front row of the grid their protests stopped. Bruce was in fourth place when a con-rod broke in the engine. At Watkins Glen a water hose blew off and in Mexico Bruce finished thirteenth and last after chronic problems with overheating.

4 Kings of CanAm

The lack of success in the 1966 CanAm races and the late delivery of the BRM V12 engine that crippled the 1967 Formula 1 programme had a direct bearing on the overwhelming success of the M6A CanAm sports cars for 1967. It was, in fact, the turning-point for Team McLaren fortunes.

Design and building had been completed on the cars for Formula 1 and Formula 2 and there was time for long involved discussions on an ideal CanAm car with Robin, Bruce, Teddy, Tyler and Wally. They analysed the reasons for their lack of success in the past, they talked about the better points of their opposition, and they went deeply into the most intimate details of a new sports car before a line was ever put on paper. They experimented with clay models seeking the optimum in aerodynamics, and worked on the full-size M1B in a wind tunnel. There were a lot of reasons contributing to the instant success of the new car. It was a monocoque for the first time, they were using Goodyear in place of Firestone tyres, the ZF had been replaced by a Hewland transmission, Lucas fuel injection was fitted for the first time to the 5.9 litre cast iron Chevrolet engines, and Denny Hulme had joined the team.

The first car – M6A-1 – was completed and ready for testing at Goodwood on June 19, more than three months prior to the opening races in the CanAm series. The car covered over 2,000 miles of testing before Elkhart Lake where Denny immediately underlined the potential of the M6A by knocking ten seconds off the old lap record in practice and then winning the race.

The best testing time round Goodwood early that season stood to Surtees in his Lola at 1min 16sec and the best lap by the M1 had been 1min 18sec. That first afternoon with the M6 running on a 200-mile destruction test without the body fitted, Bruce was lapping at 1min 16.2sec.

'For a completely new car the M6A wasn't really new,' Bruce said at the time. 'With the exception of the drive-shafts everything else was a development of something we had done before. The basic layout of the rear bulkhead was identical to that of the new M5 Formula 1 car. The idea of tying the side-stress boxes into the front engine mounts came from the 2-litre BRM-engined car. The front suspension was a mixture of the production sports car and last year's Formula 1. The scheme for the Lucas fuel injection on the Chevy engine came mainly from the M4 Formula 2 car. Our design philosophy? Simplicity, light weight, and a rider that I stressed fairly hard – strength.'

They might not have been new ideas but they were proven developments and the ideas were well tested before the series started.

'You've got to demoralise 'em right away,' Denny said when he came back from slicing the ten seconds off the old lap record at Elkhart Lake, and then Bruce went out to chop a further tenth off his time and take pole. They were two seconds faster than the next man, Dan Gurney in his Lola.

'Denny charged off into the lead from the rolling start with my car tucked in behind him,' Bruce wrote. 'I did precisely three laps. I'd lost oil from an oil cooler leak. I didn't know whether to cry, shoot myself, hurl rocks at the Lolas, or what. . . . Eventually I settled for walking back to the pits, sitting there getting more and more nervous inventing problems that might cost Denny his lead, and biting my nails down to the wrist. But this time Lady Luck was with us – believe me, she's the best pit popsy a team could have!'

At Bridgehampton Denny won again with Bruce second. At Mosport they finished 1–2 again, but the results did not begin to tell the story of the race.

'An hour before the race the mechanics went to lower my car off its jack stands when the leak appeared. The car had been sitting with full tanks since early morning. If we'd found the leak ten minutes earlier it wouldn't have been dramatic – ten minutes later and it would have been like forget it. Fifty gallons is an awful lot of petrol. Getting it out of the tanks involved filling every vehicle we had around and some we didn't. When we got to the stage of pumping it out faster than we could empty the cans into the trucks and cars, we simply tipped it over the fence. By the time we had fitted a new rubber fuel bag, filled the tanks and got the engine running, the race had started. Just forty seconds earlier, to be precise! This was just the exact gap that could be made up without going completely crazy. I made it to second place with just ten laps left. Denny was well out in front but two laps from the flag he had an incident at the hairpin and ploughed off the road, folding the left front corner in on the wheel. The fibreglass cut the tyre and it went flat, but Denny limped in with smoke pouring from the demolished front end to win. Another lap and I would have caught him. . . .'

Bruce was wistful about not catching Denny because he had yet to win a CanAm race and Denny had won three in a row. Laguna Seca was to be Bruce's race, but he almost cooked in the cockpit and half-way through the race he slowed beside the pits and the mechanics tossed a bucket of water over him. Revived, he continued to finish and win the race but his hands were blistered and his lips and mouth were badly sunburned where he had pulled his face-mask down to gasp for air.

Riverside made it two in a row for Bruce but he had to work hard for his prize money and the pace car. Gurney led for the first two of the sixty-two laps while Bruce battled with Parnelli Jones' Lola-Ford. An unintentional result of this tussle was Denny's retirement. Jones ploughed through a tyre marker knocking it out in front of Denny and the nose of the McLaren was smashed in. He raced for the pits and the crew dragged the smashed fibreglass clear of the wheel, but the officials black-flagged him and his race was over.

With Jones now behind him Bruce's next challenge came from Jim Hall in the Chaparral and the pair drove hard, swapping the lead in tail-end traffic, with each man giving of his best. This was real racing with McLaren out to beat Hall, and both men out to prove their own motorcars. As the white and orange cars came nose to tail up from Turn 9, Denny watched from the pits and wondered whether Bruce would be able to stand the pace in the desert heat.

'Bruce had been really whacked at Laguna Seca and I was sure that he was starting to tire and Jim would get the jump on him, but ten laps from the end Bruce perked up and it was all over as far as Jim was concerned.'

As they flew to Las Vegas for the final race of the '67 Series Bruce led Denny by three points for the Championship. Bruce took pole position in practice but on race morning he came in after a few warm-up laps and the mechanics found oil foam puffing out of the engine breather. It was too late to change engines – there wasn't even time to take the heads off, so they crossed their fingers and slurped in as much gasket sealing cement as they could find. It looked as though Bruce had lost his chance for the title before the race had started.

It was a moment he remembered well. 'When the race started I could barely see for oil. I let Denny by and hoped the oil problem would cure itself but then I saw Denny's left rear tyre starting to go soft. Within a couple of laps I had to stop too – by that time the oil was cooling the engine and the water was lubricating it! Denny had changed a wheel and charged out again a lap behind the leaders. All the previous hot shots – Gurney, Jones and Hall – had dropped out and Donohue was leading from Surtees and Spence. There was a chance that Denny could catch them. For an hour or more he kept picking them up at a second lap, but then his engine blew spectacularly right in front of the grandstand in a spray of water and a cloud of oil smoke that signalled the demise of that engine as well.

'If Denny's engine had held together and he had finished in a place he could have been CanAm champion in addition to being World Champion in Formula 1 that year. As it turned out, I won the CanAm championship from Denny with both of us standing in the pits as Surtees took the lead on the last lap to win. It's not the way I would have chosen to win the title, but I really can't complain. In the six CanAm races our team collected six fastest laps, qualified six times on the front row, took five pole positions, and won five races. . . .'

During the 1967 CanAm series Robin Herd had been over for some of the races, but he was working on the design basis for a new Formula 1 car rather than a development of the sports car. This was to be the M7A. Structurally it bore quite a resemblance to the monocoque M4A Formula 2 car which was elegant if not particularly successful. The M7 was in fact designed to take a chassis-mounted wing but it didn't race with a wing until the middle of 1968 after Ferrari and Brabham had used wings at Spa. Herd copied the Lotus layout by using the Ford-Cosworth V8 as a stressed member of the car and in its original test form it weighed just 30 lbs over the limit. When the design of the Formula 1 car was finished, Herd left the McLaren team to join Cosworth Engineering.

Gordon Coppuck was now chief design engineer, later being joined by Jo Marquart and in the Spring of 1968 they started the design of the M8A which followed the thinking behind the M7A single-seater in that the engine was a stress-carrying part of the car. This was more difficult because while the Ford-Cosworth had been designed to take stresses, special mounting arrangements had to be made for the 7-litre aluminium Chevrolet that the team were to use in CanAm racing during 1968. They were starting the new season with the best engines for both categories of racing and they were to make good use of them.

Bruce was now very much the manufacturer and businessman as well as a successful racing driver. He had moved from the apartment in Surbiton to a new split-level home in Weybridge with Patty and their baby daughter Amanda and the E Type Jaguar had been replaced by a 220S Mercedes coupé.

In a weak moment during negotiations for the BRM V12 engine the year before Bruce had agreed to drive a $2\frac{1}{2}$-litre

BRM on the Tasman series and this turned out to be a disaster. The cars were hopelessly uncompetitive and Bruce, normally placid and unwilling to criticize publicly other people's motorcars, was being quoted in the Auckland newspapers saying how poor his chances looked for the Grand Prix.

The V12 was said to be giving 330 horsepower equal with the Tasman version of the Ford, but Bruce offered to eat every horse that the V12 was giving in excess of 300. In an attempt to track down fuel pressure problems Bruce was lapping Pukekohe with a fuel pressure gauge sprouting between his legs. 'Most racing cars I've driven have had these sort of things mounted on the dash panel,' was the McLaren comment.

Bruce gave BRM their only win in the Series in pouring rain at Teretonga when most of the drivers went off the road at some stage. Bruce had smashed in the nose of the BRM during a preliminary heat, but it was repaired in time for the race and for once he benefited from the gentle torque and motored home to win. The next major win for BRM came when Pedro Rodriguez won the Belgian Grand Prix at Spa in 1970, a week after Bruce's death.

At home – he had now made up his mind that England was to be 'home' in the foreseeable future – Bruce had the new power of the Ford Formula 1 engine to look forward to. Denny had now officially joined the team and their first Formula 1 race with the M7s was the Race of Champions at Brands Hatch. Bruce won and Denny was third. The next event was the International Trophy at Silverstone where Denny won, Bruce was second and Chris Amon was third in the Ferrari. It was an eventful race because Denny had dropped back at half distance when a stone smashed one lens out of his goggles, but he re-took the lead and won driving with one eye shut! Chris had been challenging Bruce for second place but with only a few laps to go the strap of his goggles broke and he dropped back wrestling with his spare pair, leaving the two McLarens in a safe 1-2.

They had won the two opening races of the season but it was not a happy time for the Grand Prix 'circus'. Bruce had been

roped in to drive the new F3L Ford prototype using the 3-litre
Formula 1 engine at Brands Hatch in the BOAC 500 sports car
race, but after fighting his way into the lead the car quit and he
set off for home along the A25. On the way the news came over
his car radio that Jimmy Clark had been killed in the Formula 2
race at Hockenheim that afternoon.

'I was stunned,' Bruce wrote in his *Autosport* column. 'Jimmy
ranked with, perhaps even out-ranked Nuvolari, Fangio and
Moss, and I think we all felt that he was in a way invincible. To
be killed in an accident with a Formula 2 car is almost unaccep-
table. But tragically it's true.'

This was the way the motor racing world accepted the news
of Bruce's own death in his testing accident two years later.
Bruce did not dwell on sentimentality or talk about the risks of
his occupation, but when Jimmy was killed Bruce was moved to
put his thoughts on paper.

'Too often in this demanding sport unique in terms of ability,
dedication, concentration, and courage, someone pays the
penalty for trying to do just that little bit better or go that little
bit faster. And too often someone pays the penalty for being in
the wrong place at the wrong time when a situation or set of
circumstances is such that no human being can control them.
However, that's the way it is. We accept it, we enjoy what we do,
we get a lot of satisfaction out of it, and maybe we prove something, I don't know. . . .'

The first Grand Prix in Europe was on the new Jarama track
just outside Madrid in Spain. Denny had driven the BRM-
engined car earlier in South Africa and he finished fifth two laps
behind Clark and Hill in the Ford-engined Lotuses. With the
Ford-engined M7 McLaren Denny was second to Hill in Spain,
and at Monaco he was fifth after stopping to change a driveshaft.
Bruce's season had been dismal. He was in New Zealand with
the BRM while Denny was in South Africa, in Spain he had
been in third place when his engine started spewing oil thirteen
laps from home, and at Monaco he was out of the race on the
opening lap when he crashed after spinning on oil.

But he made up for it at Spa by winning the Belgian Grand Prix. As he crossed the finishing line and took the flag Bruce was delighted with his performance. He braked hard after crossing the line and steered through the gates at the bottom of the pits when Cyril Atkins, one of the BRM mechanics, came up and started talking excitedly to him. Bruce couldn't hear what he was saying. 'You crossed the line number one!' he shouted, but Bruce stared blankly at him. 'My number was five – I wasn't quite sure what he was on about, but then he shouted "You've won! Didn't you know?" I didn't, and it's about the nicest thing I've ever been told.' He thought he had finished second! He wasn't aware that Jackie Stewart's Matra had stopped on the last lap for more fuel, and that he had actually won his first Grand Prix in his own car.

At Colnbrook Gordon and Jo were completing the new M8A which was in effect a M6A that had been chopped off behind the rear bulkhead. Jo had been detailed to handle the design of the front end which required a tidy-up of the Herd M6A work, while Gordon did the more complicated mounting of the engine, and the rear suspension which was hung off the Hewland transmission.

The lightweight 7-litre engines were being developed by Gary Knutson and Colin Beanland in workshops in Los Angeles, but they were to experience trouble with their new dry-sump modifications and although Team McLaren orange cars won four of the six races in the series, they were less than happy with the engines. The aluminium engine weighed about the same as the cast iron version they had used the previous season but it was putting out an extra 100 horsepower.

The M8A was four inches wider than the M6A, and because of the dry-sump mods the engine sat five inches lower. The Hewland had been altered from a 5-speed to a 4-speed since a very low first gear was not required with the CanAm rolling starts.

At Elkhart Lake Bruce qualified on the pole and finished second to Denny. Bridgehampton was won by Mark Donohue in Penske's M6B, Denny and Bruce finished 1–2 at Edmonton, John Cannon won the wet Laguna Seca race in his aged McLaren Mk 2 (the production version of the M1B), Bruce won Riverside from Donohue (Denny finished fifth after stopping to have crash damage repaired), and once again they went to Las Vegas still not knowing who was going to win the Championship. Denny had a 3-point lead over Bruce and Mark who were equal in second place. Qualifying saw Bruce on pole ahead of Denny and Jim Hall with Donohue fourth. Poor Mark's car refused to start as the field fired up for the pace lap.

Bruce wrote: 'Someone said there was white smoke coming out of the exhaust pipes as Mark's engine churned over – and someone else said there was white smoke coming out of Roger's ears!'

The field bunched as they came up to the start line and in the drag race to the fast right-hand sweep of the first corner Denny pulled ahead of Bruce. Mario Andretti tried to follow Denny through from the outside but as he swept across the line he caught the nose of Bruce's car and spun him into the sand on the inside. Instantly there were cars spinning in all directions crashing into each other and slamming off the guardrailing on the outside of the corner as they ploughed blindly through the blanket of dust and sand. Miraculously nobody was hurt and as the sand settled cars were sorting themselves out and picking their way through the debris. Chris Amon's Ferrari had gone straight ahead into the dust and stayed there in the desert with the fuel injection hopelessly clogged with sand.

On the inside of the track Bruce's car front was badly battered. 'I had stalled the engine and before I came to a stop I snicked the lever into low gear, let the clutch in and the engine started. That was a surprise. When I drove back on to the track and pointed it at the first corner it went through with no drama and I was even more surprised. The brakes worked and everything felt fine, but it had been a very bumpy ride for a few seconds and I felt sure something had to be bent. I continued round and stopped at the pits yelling at the boys to have a pull at the wheels. We had a spare body available but from where I was sitting everything looked okay so I charged out again.

'But right away I knew I had made a mistake. As soon as I got up to any sort of speed the nose shell started to lift so that at the end of that lap I came back into the pits, they lifted the shattered nose shell off, dropped the new one on, tied it tight with tape and rubber cords, and I charged off. It was the third time I'd started this race!' He had to start a fourth time when he was black-flagged for having no mirrors on the new nose, and he finally finished the race drastically slowed when a brake seal blew out and he lost all the brakes. In the closing laps he was cruising past the pits shouting an unintelligible message to the crew. They did not know he was without brakes until he came in after the race and almost wiped everyone out because he could not stop!

In that race Jim Hall broke both his legs when his Chaparral flipped over the back of a car that suddenly slowed in front of him.

Denny took the CanAm title in 1968 with Bruce second; they had taken pole position in all six races and McLaren cars had won all six, but it was not until the last couple of races that they had managed to get on top of their engine problems.

In Formula 1 they were on the crest of a wave. At Monza Bruce had qualified second fastest to Surtees' Honda and he was sitting in the middle of the front row with John on one side and Chris Amon's Ferrari on the other. Bruce made a perfect start with the rev counter needle firmly on nine-eight and he grabbed a handy lead in the opening laps. On lap Eight Amon had taken Surtees for second place but then the Ferrari slid wide, hit the guardrails and somersaulted backwards into the trees while Surtees smashed into the guardrails trying to dodge the spinning Ferrari. Chris was saved by his seat harness.

Bruce was caught a few laps later by the usual Monza bunch of slipstreamers and he dropped back to retire finally with an oil leak, but Denny took over to trade blows with Stewart's Matra until Jackie's engine blew and Denny led for the remaining twenty-eight laps.

In Canada for the Grand Prix the McLaren team turned on a CanAm performance finishing first and second with Denny leading over the line and boosting his Championship score to equal Graham Hill in the lead. The race really belonged to Amon's Ferrari which had equalled Rindt's pole position time and led for seventy-two of the ninety laps, dropping out with a broken transmission when almost a lap ahead of Denny's McLaren. But it proved the old motor racing maxim: To finish first, first you must finish.

Dan Gurney had been driving a third McLaren at Ste Jovite and he led the other works cars early in the race until forced to retire with overheating. Dan drove his rented McLaren again at Watkins Glen and was running third until a puncture two laps from the flag dropped him to fourth. Denny had crashed and Bruce had run short of fuel with a blocked tank breather.

Denny stood a chance of retaining his Championship title down at Mexico City but that chance vanished when his rear suspension snapped coming into the pit straight and he crashed into the barrier, skidding down past the pits on three wheels and clambering out hurriedly as a blaze around the engine was quelled by fire-fighters. Bruce came in second to Hill's Lotus as Graham clinched his second World championship in what had been a black year for Lotus with Jimmy's death.

Denny had finished third in the Championship and Bruce was fifth, but in the constructor's championship McLaren cars were second on points behind Lotus and when they got back to England there was a surprise waiting for Bruce. It had been decided he was to be awarded the Ferodo Trophy 'for his tenacity of purpose in making and developing cars which have won Formula 1 Grands Prix, and Group 7 cars which have dominated the CanAm championship'. In his reply on behalf of the team after receiving the celebrated golden spike from the chairman of Ferodo, Bruce said, 'I would like to think the company couldn't have done the job without me, but I know that I certainly couldn't have done the job without them.'

Bruce's eloquence came as a surprise to some, but he had been getting plenty of practice as a 'star' in America and he was certainly a better known personality there than he was in Europe. Jim Kaser, the man mainly responsible for setting up the CanAm series as Director of Professional Racing for the Sports Car Club of America, gave McLaren the man as much credit for the success of the CanAm series as he gave McLaren the driver and McLaren the car-builder. Bruce worked hard to ensure the success of the Series but at times he was over-working himself and this showed. 'I remember how bloody tired he used to get,' says Kaser. 'He would really run himself down with a very ambitious programme and I remember him dragging himself off aeroplanes and getting out to the CanAm race that weekend, trying to grab some sleep, and then on Monday morning he's on that jet again going back to England. But he was the nicest guy. He could really relax alongside the motel pool to get away from the pressures of the moment. He was a nice guy when he needed to be in front of the television cameras or the Press, but he was just the same anywhere else, and that's the sort of things you remember about an individual – what he was like when he wasn't up front, when he didn't have to turn it on. . . .'

As the team grew and the cars became more and more successful, Bruce's schedule became busier and busier. Although his leg sometimes bothered him when he was tired, and occasionally he talked of having an operation done on the hipjoint, he was immensely strong and was able to stand the strain of the constant travel probably better than Denny or Teddy. One eye was quite a bit weaker than the other, to the point where he would fake the eye test at the track medicals, covering the weak eye with his right hand to read the chart and then using his left hand to cover the same eye and read the chart again. He wasn't able to fake the Indianapolis medical this way, but on the day his eye was strong enough to pass their test. When he was tired it seemed to be worse, but few people were aware of it. He had the ability to relax completely and sleep anywhere which helped to conserve his energy, and he also worked-out on a trampoline in his garden whenever he had a chance.

For 1969 the M8B CanAm car was an updated version of the M8A with a high wing mounted to the rear uprights, and the Formula 1 car was updated to M7C and followed the design of the M10 Formula A/5,000 car with a full monocoque instead of the open-topped 'bathtub'. The spate of accidents with wings early in 1969 resulted in the sudden wing ban at Monaco in May and this accelerated development of 4-wheel-drive cars in the Lotus, Matra and McLaren camps. At Cosworth Robin Herd was designing a completely new car around 4-wheel-drive, but it was destined never to race. In fact the 4-wheel-drive programme was a dead-end road for all concerned, and for Lotus and McLaren it resulted in a season of lost development with all the design and development efforts wasted on 4-wheel-drive cars.

Bruce finished third in the 1969 World championship behind Jackie Stewart's Matra and Jacky Ickx's Brabham. His best placing was a second in the Spanish GP at Barcelona after the Team Lotus wing accidents had demolished the cars of Hill and Rindt. Stewart was the king that season with six wins in the eleven Grands Prix with the Tyrrell-entered Matra.

Denny finished a lowly sixth in the world title but he scored a convincing win in the final race of the season at Mexico. It was a mixture of determination and supreme confidence. Denny had qualified beside Stewart's Matra on the second row of the grid and from the start he had passed Brabham on lap 6, Stewart on lap 8, and on the tenth lap he had taken Ickx for the lead which he held to the end.

It was the last race of the 1960s and it was more than significant that while a youthful Bruce McLaren had won the first race of the decade in Argentina, one of his Grand Prix cars had won the final race in Mexico. It spelt the switch from the factory drivers to the driver/constructors with first Brabham, then Gurney and McLaren and later Surtees deciding that they could build better cars themselves.

The CanAm series that season had gone pretty much according to what people felt was the McLaren Plan. They won all
eleven races, with Bruce taking the chequer in six and winning
the Championship for the second time.

They had the M15 Indianapolis car ready for testing in
November, and the 1970 M14 Formula 1 car was being built
alongside it, being an improved version of the M7 and its
derivatives with a better suspension layout. In 1970 McLaren
Racing was to be the only team taking part in CanAm,
Indianapolis, and Grand Prix racing, and Bruce was considering starting to phase himself out from the chore of driving every
weekend. He had decided to drop Formula 1 personally and
concentrate on development but he wanted to stay in CanAm
racing. At Watkins Glen in 1969 Bruce talked with Jochen
Rindt, Jackie Stewart and Chris Amon asking if there was any
way they could get together to drive with Denny in the McLaren
Formula 1 team. Jochen was sorely tempted to sign with
McLaren for 1970, but Bruce did not want to run three CanAm
sports cars and, as Jochen said, 'they would have been keeping
me away from the bread . . .'.

It would be pleasant to think that if Jochen had signed with
the McLaren team, both he and Bruce would be alive today
but the sad fact is that Bruce revelled so much in testing that his
accident in the new finned M8D was almost inevitable.

5 McLaren Design and Designers

In the field of detail design in motor racing the fact that the Dzus fastener had not been properly clipped to close the hatch in the nose of the Zerex Special was probably as significant as the apple falling on Isaac Newton's head. Bruce was testing the Zerex at Goodwood and soon after leaving the pits he realized that the small flap-like hatch to the oil tank had come undone. He decided to stop and fix it next time round. As he tooled round the tight right-hander at Lavant and motored out on to the straight picking up speed he mused absently on the fact that the forward-hinged flap was being forced up and open the faster he went instead of being flattened shut with the force of the airstream over the sleek nose of the Zerex. That inconsistency set McLaren's mind in mesh and by the time he had reached the pits he wasn't looking for a screwdriver – he wanted a pair of tin snips! He expounded his new theory to the mechanics and soon he had hacked a sizeable hole in the nose of the car, centring on where the oil tank hatch had been. This tin snippery did little for the looks on the car, but in his first fast laps Bruce realized he had accidently stumbled on the answer to several of their handling problems at high speed.

At the time, late in 1964, there were very few applications of aerodynamic theory (being applied) to racing cars, and a smooth wind-cheating shape that looked right was regarded as the optimum. The Zerex with more power from the 3.9 litre Oldsmobile V8 in place of the 2.7 litre 4-cylinder Coventry Climax engine found itself with a problem of understeer and instability at high speed because the nose was getting light. Air taken in through the intake in the front of the nose was passed through the core of the radiator and left to find its own method of exit under the car, and this caused a pressure area that lifted the nose at high speed. When the flap opened in the nose of the Zerex and Bruce realized that the air pressure coming up from inside the nose was greater than the force of airstream he knew he was on to something important. The larger hole he hacked in the nose was a crude fore-runner of the distinctive 'nostrils' that have been a feature of all McLaren cars since then, and are now also common to most other racing cars in all fields.

Bruce had the three years he spent studying for his engineering degree in Auckland as a base of theory, and he built on to this base with years of practical experience in the motor racing field. To begin with he learned about racing from his father, but when he first arrived in England in 1958 it was Jack Brabham's coaching and coaxing, together with McLaren's own racing talent, that earned him a spot in the Cooper Formula 1 works team in 1959.

From Cooper and from Brabham, Bruce learned that development on an established theme was often better than innovation for the sake of innovation. Brabham pursued this theory when he left the Cooper team building workmanlike straightforward cars with Ron Tauranac that set few standards in advanced racing design, but they were race winners and they sold like hot cakes. As an example of the Brabham refusal to follow the herd, they continued to build space-frame cars ignoring the aluminium monocoques in use by all other teams until they finally brought out their monocoque BT33 in 1970. Ron Tauranac used to maintain that the fastest thing about a monocoque was Jimmy Clark.

The first McLaren sports cars were very obviously Cooper-based with McLaren ideas superimposed, and it was not until Robin Herd joined the team bringing with him advanced – and not always practical – theories from the Royal Aircraft Establishment, that the true McLaren stamp became apparent. Their first Formula 1 car was so bundled up with accumulated ideas on how to go Grand Prix racing with a brand new car that it was little better than a failure. The main cause of the disastrous uncompetitiveness of the M2B was the dead weight of the 3-litre version of the 4-cam Indianapolis V8 engine, but in other areas the car also ignored later McLaren principles of developing an established theme. The lesson was learned well.

Looking back, Herd remembers that their thinking when he joined the team early in 1965 was very much influenced by Jim Hall and his Chaparrals. 'Jim was going through a phase of being a really outstanding designer and constructor and our emphasis tended to be more on the elegance of the chassis structure rather than on the design of a really quick racing car. I now find this rather surprising because Bruce's sense of values in relation to the design and engineering of a racing car was first class. He never, after our first few months together anyway, lost sight of the immediate aim which was to design a car which crossed the finishing line first. On our initial design we erred from this and tended to go towards technical ingenuity and bullshit rather than racewinning engineering.'

Herd had been hired as an enthusiastic new 'brain' who had come down from Oxford with an engineering degree and had been hired by the Royal Aircraft Establishment to work in the National Gas Turbine Establishment at Farnborough as a scientific officer on the Concorde project. As a racing car designer Herd was 'green' when he arrived at McLaren's and to begin with he and Bruce operated very much like a Y, with Bruce and Robin on opposite sides pooling the knowledge from their different fields and joining at the fork with a cohesive design. Towards the end of 1965 the McLaren design team was joined by another Farnborough man. Gordon Coppuck had been a leading draughtsman at the N.G.T.E. and had worked with Herd. When Robin left to join Cosworth Engineering at the end of 1968 it was Gordon who became chief designer.

'Bruce was very good at vehicle dynamics,' says Gordon. 'This is the theory of why vehicles do certain things – vehicles generally, and not just racing cars. Whereas most racing drivers could tell you whether the car was oversteering or understeering Bruce understood about centres of gravity, moments of inertia, and things of that nature – and he could apply these. This was something that was of great benefit to the firm. I don't know where he learned it, or whether he just evolved it himself. I don't think he would have learned it at school because it isn't taught in schools. He most likely evolved it by applying a basically good education and a good mind.'

Robin Herd recalls that Bruce had a big influence on the way he carried out his detail design but he also feels that to a degree he changed Bruce's thinking. 'Bruce's designs would tend to be very easy to make, sound, reliable, perhaps not very light, and I think it's fair to say not particularly elegant, whereas mine were the other way round. Between us we made up for each other's deficiencies by our experience and ability such as it was then. Bruce gave me an immensely free hand in the design and when I talk to other people – like the way Maurice Philipe works with Colin Chapman at Lotus – I realize just how good Bruce was in this way, although perhaps I didn't fully appreciate it at the time. He had the experience I hadn't got and he really was a super bloke to work with.'

Herd maintains that although he and Gordon looked after the detail design and Bruce would come by every couple of weeks between races to check and maybe change something, Bruce could have carried out this detail design himself but he was prevented from doing so by lack of time. 'If he changed something it was always for a valid reason. He did have one or two idiosyncracies, but eventually one got to know what these were, and one avoided incorporating them in the design.'

Herd's background in advanced design spurred the interest and development of the McLaren team in the field of aerodynamics, and they were experimenting with the wings and adjustable tail-fins back in 1965.

The tyre-test car, the M2A Mallite chassis car fitted with an Oldsmobile sports car engine as a test vehicle both for Firestone and as a prototype Formula 1 car for the Formula change in 1966, was taken to Zandvoort in November 1965 and a simple sort of wing was tried on the back. With the wing fitted Bruce immediately chopped three seconds off his lap time and with the wing removed his times fell back by the same three seconds. All evidence of the wing was then destroyed as the team determined to use it as their secret weapon for 1966. 'Indeed if the Indy Ford engine had lived up to expectations you would have seen the M2B McLaren with a wing on the back,' says Herd.

The problems with the underpowered overweight Ford engine effectively cancelled early McLaren experiments with wings and fins because the M2A prototype used the 4-cam Ford for tyre testing at Riverside early in 1966 and the car was fitted up to carry an advanced form of adjustable wing mounted above the transmission. It was designed so that the angle could be altered to suit the amount of downthrust required, but engine trouble curtailed these wing tests. The fact that Dan Gurney was sitting on the pit wall during much of the testing also had a negative effective on the production of new ideas before such an interested spectator.

Herd outlines the basic theory of aerodynamics as applied to racing cars. 'Our ignorance of aerodynamics is vast, but this is where the biggest gain in racing car design is going to come. If we only had a bit more knowledge and some sensible research was done we could improve the aerodynamics enormously. We're after low drag so that we can gain acceleration and maximum speed, but we also want negative lift which has the effect of pushing the car down on the ground, increasing the cornering force and traction in proportion to the force between the tyre and the road. This force between the tyre and the road comes from two factors: the first is the weight of the car, and the second is the aerodynamic downforce on the car. If you can use aerodynamics to increase this downforce you can increase traction in braking and cornering immensely.'

As an example of early efforts at aerodynamic in racing, Herd points to the streamlined Cooper at Rheims. 'I'm sure Brabham would never dream of using a body like that now on one of his cars. Unfortunately they tried something that was a sensible experiment and it didn't work so they said that the basic idea was wrong and scrapped the whole thing. 'The basic idea wasn't wrong. What was wrong was the detail interpretation of the idea. The particular body-shape they tried was wrong. You know, I look at a photograph of that car now, and I think "Jesus – poor Jack, he must have had the fright of his life. . . ." '

The McLaren M1A, the very first McLaren sports car that was built late in 1964, had an attractive body-shape with low drag, but it was like a mobile wing the wrong way up and it developed a tremendous amount of lift. It was quick in a straight line, but it was not very quick round corners. The M2B sports car the following year was essentially a revised and improved M1A and one of the big gains with the 1965 car was the new body-shape which had been styled by Michael Turner to the aerodynamic requirements of the McLaren designers. Herd rates the M1B McLaren as one of the most attractive body styles ever on a two-seater sports car.

Experiments on aerodynamics in a wind tunnel told only half the story, because a wind tunnel cannot reproduce road conditions. The ride height varies considerably in cornering, braking, accelerating and at speed, and this has a big effect on the aerodynamics. 'We tried wind tunnel work on the early sports cars,' says Herd, 'and we came up with a whole string of answers most of which were wrong in terms of the car's performance on the track. In order to obtain realistic data we went down to Goodwood with the M6A and set up a series of pressure tappings over the internal and external surfaces of the car, and I rode as passenger to record the appropriate readings.'

In another test at Goodwood, Herd rode as passenger sprawled out from the cockpit facing backwards over the tail so that he could watch the behaviour of the rear suspension through holes in the body to try and trace the problem with the handling. During this test, Robin's legs slid across Bruce's left arm pinning it in the middle of a corner and they spun down the road. Robin, facing backwards, could do nothing about the situation except hang on for dear life! 'Looking back on this incident as the car got steadily more out of shape I am surprised to recall a feeling of calmness rather than terror, and having enough time to convince myself that if Bruce couldn't get us out of this situation, nobody could. It was fascinating to see the combination of throttle bursts, steering movements and brake applications that sent us spinning harmlessly down the centre of the track. When the car stopped we both looked at each other and started hooting with laughter. I'm not sure now whether I was laughing from amusement or sheer relief . . .'

Although the actual design of the McLaren cars was put on paper in the drawing office by Robin Herd and Gordon Coppuck, the initial design discussions when details of a new car or a development of a previous model were hammered out, were long involved conversations between the designers and Bruce, Teddy, Tyler and Don Beresford who was in charge of construction of the new cars. With design and the build programme completed, the development of the new car then depended very much on the test driver and his ability to iron out the bugs.

Test driving was something Bruce revelled in for it was, to him, an enjoyable extension of all his engineering training combined with the pursuit of what had started out as his hobby – racing. The McLaren talents as a tester did not only benefit his own team. When Ford decided to go racing with the GT40s that grew from Eric Broadley's original mid-engined Lola GT, Bruce was retained as a development driver and he worked with the company during much of the project. In 1966 he won the Le Mans 24-hour race in one of the Fords that he helped to develop, co-driving with Chris Amon. Roy Lunn, then in charge of the GT40 programme for Ford, remembers the early tests on the GT40 when Bruce and Phil Hill were driving for Ford. 'There was a real contrast between them. Phil would come in and say *everything* was wrong with the car, but Bruce was such a nice guy that he didn't like to criticize the car, so you had to dilute everything Phil said by a factor of ten, and accentuate everything Bruce said that was slightly derogatory about the car by an equal factor the other way. Bruce went from that stage to being a very objective guy in every respect of testing.

He would come in with the car after a test run and tell you exactly what had happened, and what's more he could tell you what to do to put it right. He was just a wonderful combination of driver and engineer and car builder and he could also communicate with you. I think that was the success of his cars. He had all three, and minimum communications problems because they were all locked into one guy. That was the problem we had. If we were designing and building a car, we weren't capable of driving and testing so we had to rely on the test driver to communicate back. Bruce was able to communicate back – he could tell you you had a problem and also how to cure it.'

Chuck Mountain, who also worked on the Ford racing project, agreed. 'That was beautiful. So many guys go out and have a problem and they have difficulty enough in just defining it, but Bruce could perceive the problem, define it, and have half a dozen solutions by the time he pulled back to the pits. He'd pick up the most uncanny things – things that were just so remote that you wouldn't think a guy had the ability to feel or recognize them, but you would check into what he said and make a change and sure'n Hell he was right!'

In 1964 when the GT40s went to Le Mans for the first time, Bruce's car developed an electrical miss on the last night of practice when he was up around 160mph on the straight. The engine would mysteriously drop 300rpm and the technicians checked and double-checked and by the time they had finished practice had ended and there was no further chance to try the car before the race. Bruce offered to drive Lunn back to the hotel and garage at La Charte about twenty miles from the circuit, so that he could satisfy himself that the problem had or had not been fixed. 'It was about 11.30 at night going across the rolling French countryside and it was the most hairy ride I've ever had in my life. By the time we got it up to 160mph he leaned over and shouted "Can you hear it missing?" Hear it missing – Man, I was hearing angels singing . . .!'

Bruce's 1966 Le Mans win was his high point in the association with Ford, although he could never come to terms with the enormity of the whole operation which descended on Le Mans like an invasion and won the race almost by overpowering it in the early attempts. Bruce loved the story of the 1964 race when Phil Hill made a panic pit stop on the very first lap with a misfiring engine. Phil, never one to stand quietly about in moments of tension, was shouting his problem to the team management while the engine cover was being hinged back. He felt sure the problem was a blocked jet, and since there was a different expert for every aspect of the car, the call went out for the carburettor man. He was nowhere to be found, until a shrill little voice was heard from the balcony above the pits. The carburettor man's work was apparently presumed completed when the race started and since there had not been enough pit passes to go round, he had been relegated to the grandstand!

For the Ford men, Bruce's best race was the Le Mans he did not win in 1967 when Dan Gurney and A. J. Foyt came home first in their Mk2GT. Lunn takes up the story, 'Gurney and Foyt have to be, from my point of view, the worst development drivers when it comes to setting up a car, and to have the two of them in one car both with different ideas of how the car should be set up . . . they got the car really screwed up on the two days of practice just getting progressively worse.' Mountain said Dan and A.J. almost had reached the point of deciding to go out and blow the car early in the race. 'They were going to give it a clutch job on the back straight or something. That was the point they'd gotten to on the night before the race.' Lunn continued, 'They had got their car to go progressively slower and slower while Bruce meanwhile was doing his normal routine improvements and he had the fastest qualifying time sharing the drive with Mark Donohue. Their car was beautifully set up, so what we did was to take the Gurney/Foyt car back to the garage and set it up exactly the same as Bruce's car. By the time they got into it at the beginning of the race, they'd never driven THAT car . . . it was set up completely different and of course, they went on and won the darn race!'

The ability to test drive, to be able to analyse the behaviour of a racing car at competitive track speeds, comes only from experience, and experience was something Bruce had a lot of.

Robin Herd likens test drivers in racing cars to test pilots of new aeroplanes. 'They are just as crucial to the success of the project, although this is seldom appreciated. Unfortunately there is no recognized training for a test driver and it is therefore not surprising that those who are good are also very rare. The driver has to be sensitive to the car's behaviour although there are several factors which make this difficult. It's amazing, for instance, how easy it is to become accustomed to even the most unpleasant faults in a car if one drives it for some time. You encounter this when someone new drives your own road car. Further, for each driver there appears to be certain aspects of the car's performance to which he is almost blind, so to some extent it pays to have several people test-drive a new car because you will usually learn something from each one.'

After a day testing at Goodwood the results would be examined in some depth during the drive back to the factory in Bruce's Mercedes or Zodiac with Teddy, Tyler and Robin (or later Gordon), all sharing in this rolling development session. These sessions were a most enjoyable phase of testing, remembers Robin. 'We'd go through what we had run during the day and then we would analyse what the car was doing in all aspects of its performance, why it was doing this, whether it was good or bad, and if it was bad or only adequate, what we could possibly do to improve it. It was in these head-scratching drives that we really found some big improvements in performance and these were inevitably reflected in later designs.'

Bruce's pet theories were something of a family joke within the team, and his 'whoosh-bonk' cars were typical of the McLaren tenacity to follow one of his ideas through in the face of what he considered to be ill-founded opposition. 'If Bruce had one of his theories, even if it was crazy, he was able to make it happen,' Tyler recalls. 'Everyone had a lot of faith in him and he was able to instil enthusiasm for these projects.' 'Whoosh-bonk'

came from Bruce's enthusiastic assurance of the short time the
cars would take to construct – 'You take the suspension off the
sports car – whoosh – knock up a chassis and – bonk – there's
the car!'

It was probably Patsy Burt and her garage and racing
manager, Ron Smith, who prompted the hurricane build programme on the whoosh-bonk cars that went down in the
McLaren list as the M3. In fact they were single-seater space
frame versions of the M1 sports car, just as the M15 car for
Indianapolis was in effect a single-seater version of the M8
CanAm car. The new cars, Bruce enthused, would find an
unlimited market to hillclimb and sprint specialists such as
Patsy who held most of the ladies' sprint records and a lot of hill
titles. When others in the company failed to mirror his optimism,
Bruce pressed on alone. 'It was a classic of Bruce's cigarette-
packet designing,' according to Gordon. 'Neither Robin or I
had anything to do with it. Bruce literally designed it on scraps
of paper and picked out the suspension based on the previous
year's sports car. He took these sketches to John Thompson in
the workshop and he joined up the points under Bruce's super-
vision. It all happened in a fortnight. There were no drawings,
and in fact we still don't have any drawings of the M3! After we
had built three – one for Patsy Burt, one for the Swiss hill-
climber Harry Zwiefel, and one for MGM as a camera car for
their film 'Grand Prix' – we thought perhaps someone else
might want one and so we would do a drawing of the chassis as
it was. We had a designer to draw the chassis as a "moonlight"
job, and he had no sooner finished the drawing than the cleaner
screwed it up and threw it in the waste paper, so we never did
get a proper design drawing of the M3!'

Bruce's other pet theory was the side-tank M7C version of
the M7 Formula 1 car which he had fitted with pannier fuel
tanks extending as far as the regulations would allow on either
side of the monocoque between the wheels. Tyler remembers
how it started. 'I believe it all stemmed from a discussion Bruce
had with Colin Chapman about sports cars, and Chapman

reckoned that perhaps one of the reasons that a sports car handled better than a single-seater was that the weight was spread out more instead of having all the weight on the centre of the car. Bruce had also thought about this and since he respected Chapman's opinion he seized upon this opportunity to build a single-seater with sports car characteristics. He did some initial testing with this car and it did prove to be better, but the practical applications of the thing didn't work out because it made the car too heavy and we had to abandon the project. The idea, I think, was right, and we did prove it to some extent with the M15 Indianapolis car getting the weight low and spread out between the wheels.'

Bruce's favourite project was the road-going version of the ill-fated M6GT which failed to get homologated for Group 5 as a 50-off GT car, even though a batch of 50 neat-looking GT bodies had been made to fit the basic M6 monocoque CanAm chassis. Building his own road car was a project that interested Bruce as an ambition to be achieved when the company was well under way with the racing programme. It was a sort of five-year-old project, but during the winter, early in 1970, he organized the building of one of the M6GTs to use on the road in an effort to find out what problems would have to be overcome in a proper mid-engined road GT car. The result was, literally, a semi-civilized CanAm car that was anything but easy to climb into but was bliss to drive or ride in once you were installed. Even with a cooking 5-litre Chevrolet V8 in the back it would accelerate to 100mph in around 8secs, and of course the handling was fantastic. One problem was that the car was so low that other traffic often had difficulty in seeing it coming up behind. Bruce loved the GT, but he was not blind to its shortcomings. In fact he had started work on an alternative design at the time of his death, spurred on by a very stylish artist's impression of what the McLaren road car could look like.

Gordon and Bruce had long discussions about the M6GT and about the problems they had discovered running the car on the road. The radiator outlet duct in the nose, for instance, while proving to be an ideal screen de-froster on cold mornings, generated a lot of noise and they had decided to delete the duct on the next version of a McLaren road car. Entry and exit across the broad side-tanks was another feature that was scheduled for a tidy-up. 'Another problem,' said Gordon, 'was that it had odd-sized wheels with small ones on the front and big ones on the back. It handled beautifully, but it meant that we would have to find out which were the best rim sizes so that we only needed to carry one spare wheel. At that time there wasn't room for a spare anyway, and that was another problem. I was really surprised with how comfortable the car was when I borrowed it for a weekend. Quite incredible when you considered that it was basically a racing car.'

Bruce had built up an intimate relationship with Robin, their designs were very much joint efforts, and for this reason Bruce was very hurt when Robin left to join Cosworth. He felt that Robin was taking with him all that Bruce knew in the building up of a racing car and a racing team. Strangely enough it was the same sort of hurt that Bruce could not understand with Charles and John Cooper when Jack Brabham left the Cooper team at the end of the 1961 season. Bruce always felt that while the Coopers maintained that Jack had taken all the company's racing knowledge with him, in fact Jack had done a tremendous amount for the Cooper team in return and there should have been no recriminations when he left.

Gordon noticed that, after Robin left, Bruce was reluctant to take him into his confidence on design matters because he had a sneaking suspicion that since Gordon had followed Robin from the National Gas Turbine Establishment to McLaren's, he might well follow him from the McLaren team to Cosworth. When Bruce realized that Gordon had no intentions of leaving the team, he soon came round again to building up a close liaison with his designers. Jo Marquart, a Swiss-born designer who had come from Lotus to the McLaren team, joined Gordon on the design team when Robin left at the end of the 1968 season.

Gordon had been working in Robin's shadow, and the first car he really designed was the M10A car for Formula A and Formula 5,000 racing. 'That was actually my project and Bruce was very communicative and very helpful. Obviously he knew what he wanted, but it's one thing to have had him come and say what he wanted straight out, and another thing to discuss it and evolve what seems to be the best solution to the particular problem. I'm sure he was pleased with the result of the M10 and by the time we were doing the M15 Indianapolis car I did that more on my own with more of my ideas on it than I'd been used to having. We used the expression that by then I was "McLaren-orientated". I believed that the way in which we were developing was the right way for us. It wasn't a question of just going along with what Bruce thought about any particular design feature – I really believed that for us it was the best way to do it.'

Designing is probably the least glamorous side of a racing team from the outsider's point of view, but in the world of design there is a certain amount of contained excitement in bringing a racing car concept into being via the drawing-board.

Gordon does not find his job dull. 'The thing that strikes you about racing is the speed with which drawings are turned into parts. In the Gas Turbine Establishment, I'd been used to people coming up with drawing office queries fifteen months after I'd done the drawings, and I couldn't remember anything about them. In racing, drawings become parts within a week, and that's so much more satisfying from a drawing point of view without considering the excitement of motor racing itself.

'I must confess that I don't find racing in itself as exciting as perhaps the spectators do. It's exciting to me if it is an exciting race and we are directly involved in the action, but winning a race at a canter doesn't thrill me and *not* winning a race doesn't impress me either. I think it's important for designers to go to race meetings at sufficient intervals to be aware of how the team is doing in racing. It's very easy not to go to races and keep getting secondhand stories that don't always transpire to be true, whereas if the designer is there he will know at first hand what has happened. Someone should certainly be in direct contact with people who have been to every race. To remain competitive you must have detailed knowledge of what happened last Sunday. The team manager should tell you what developments have taken place, and the chief mechanic should tell you what problems have arisen, both with our cars and with similar parts to ours on other cars.'

Bruce's overall concept of a car was important to the designers and to the concept discussions that were held either formally in Bruce's office or informally over dinner that Patty had cooked at home. Like most motor racing wives, Patty had to sit at the edge of long involved conversations keeping vague track of the topic and avoid making inane remarks.

'Bruce knew how the car should be and how it should be laid out,' says Gordon. 'He was also very good when it came to difficult details on the car. When we were doing the M8 CanAm car we came across a particular difficulty where we couldn't get a sanitary solution for the point where the tubes joined the bell-housing at the rear of the engine. Bruce could sit and nut out a problem like that, while we were getting on with the rest of the design. If something looked right, Bruce maintained that it usually *was* right, but he always followed this up by saying that if it looked wrong it was wrong. We will certainly miss Bruce's development work on a car. Having taken the car from the drawing office and made it and taken it down to Goodwood to test, he could quickly put his finger on any bugs that needed sorting out. He was able to translate these problems to us and communicate well. You could talk to him and understand what he meant and this communication between the driver and the designer (and this was probably even stronger between Bruce and Tyler) was very strong. That's where I've learned all I know about racing . . .'

6 Development of Racing Engines

The decision to use the Ford Indianapolis V8 in 3-litre form for their first Grand Prix car in 1966 cost the McLaren team dearly during the first two seasons of the new Formula. They had based their development programme around the Ford engine, but when it failed to meet hoped-for requirements the Grand Prix project virtually lost its drive for two years. And during those two years the Brabham team used the engine the McLaren team rejected – the F85 Oldsmobile with its aluminium block – to win two World championships. In 1968 the Ford Cosworth engines were made available to teams other than Lotus, and the McLaren team came back on even terms engine-wise, but they had lost two years of development while they switched from one stop-gap engine to another. They lost their early advantage in tyre technology logged during their initial testing with Firestones in 1965 and they also lost their development work on airfoils done in secret during 1965 and planned for use as a 'secret weapon' in 1966 – two full seasons before the airfoil wings first appeared on the Brabhams and Ferraris at Spa for the Belgian Grand Prix in 1968.

In April 1965 Bruce called a meeting in his office at the Feltham factory for seven o'clock one night and with Teddy Mayer, mechanics Tyler Alexander and Wally Willmott and designers Robin Herd and Eddie Stait, he discussed opinions on an engine for the new 3-litre Formula the following year. It was obviously important to strike while the iron was hot and to have a proven engine ready to race while other teams were perhaps struggling to sort out a new power unit.

They talked about the new BRM engine but it seemed wise to let BRM deal with their own teething troubles. They decided the Maserati V12 would probably be less than competitive and anyway it seemed that the Cooper team had lined up an exclusive deal with the Italian factory. The 2.7 litre Coventry Climax engine? Not enough power and not enough scope for development. A 3-litre version of the Oldsmobile engine they had been using for sports car racing? The job of engineering a conversion on the stock-block engine would be prohibitively expensive, and they were not sure that the block was strong enough to stand the higher rpm in 3-litre form.

The 4-cam Indianapolis Ford presented itself as the best choice because it was a pure racing engine and as such could be developed, and there was always a chance that the Ford Motor Company would take an active financial interest in a team who were preparing to go Grand Prix racing with a Ford engine for the first time.

'We were never under the delusion that the engine was a potential winner without major engineering changes, but we had a feeling that we might be able to pressure or coax or lead Ford into doing something about the engine for us if we were to take the initiative. But although we did get some back door advice, Ford never did get involved in any overt operation with us,' says Teddy Mayer.

In 4.2 litre form running on gasoline the 4-cam Ford was giving a reliable 470bhp, and it was felt that with the reduction in capacity to 3-litres there would be a safe 335bhp with a pleasant torque curve to start with, and more power to come with the higher revs that could be used with what was really a sophisticated racing engine.

In the light of more recent developments in the engine field, however, it is now apparent that the basic design of the heads on the Ford was wrong for a 3-litre application but expert opinion at the time deemed that the engine could be made to give the required horsepower in reduced form. Klaus von Rucker who had worked on BMW and Mercedes racing engines had been appointed as a consultant to look into the possibilities of the Ford, and engineering work started in England.

Gary Knutson soon found that progress was lagging on the engine project and the whole operation was shipped across to the workshops of Traco Engineering in Culver City, California. Five 1964 Ford Indy engines were bought from Ford. Early in 1966 the Formula 1 Indy Ford engine ran in the McLaren M2A Mallite chassis for the first time during Firestone tests at Riverside but valve problems cut the testing short. Work continued at the Traco shop where the McLaren engine men were working to sort out the several problems, and Bruce received a graphic note from Wally Willmott: 'We had decided to try dropping our valves somewhere else so we set up a cylinder head in one of Mr Nairn's (an engineering shop next door to Traco's) big machines and coupled it up with oil pumps, splash shields and loving care. The first test ran for five minutes at 10,500 revs, then broke a valve spring, just about deafened all in Mr Nairn's shop and started to eat up his big machine. The last two items didn't appeal to Mr Nairn's sense of humour so we had to revise our test rig somewhat. The gobbling of the machine was fixed quite easily but the noise factor meant we could only run at night after everyone had gone home. The final result was that in the next four days and nights we worked from 10am to 5pm at Traco's then from 5pm to 3am at Nairn Machine Co. In these four days I saw more broken valve springs and learnt more new words rude and technical than I had picked up in the last five years. The final outcome of the whole deal was that we now had a valve that has done around 1,800,000 ins-and-outs, and a valve-spring set-up that lasts for $1\frac{1}{4}$ hours at 10,500 revs. This doesn't sound like very long but it is 10,500 revs that kills the springs and when you think of the number of times and the period that an engine reaches or holds these revs even at Rheims, it isn't too bad. The valve is excellent and as it hasn't broken we could last at least a minute at 1,800,000rpm or you could work it back from there – like two minutes at 900,000rpm.'

The engine certainly looked impressive in the chassis with the big-bore injection bellmouths sticking up four on each side of the engine, and the drain-pipe pair of exhausts coming out the centre of the Vee and sloping down and back. It sounded impressive too. At Monaco the aching ear-splitting blast of noise was almost beyond comprehension as it bounced off the buildings in the Principality. But the performance was dismal. It had proved to be unbelievably heavy, unreliable, and the peak horsepower of just on 300bhp was only available in a very narrow rev range. The team had been hoping to start the season with at least 330bhp. An oil union came loose after ten laps, and Bruce's race was over.

Count Volpi, head of the Italian Serenissima Company was aware of the desperate straits of the McLaren team and he offered them the use of his 3-litre V8 sports car engine. It was giving only 260bhp, but it was an engine and it did work, and the team set about altering the chassis to fit the Serenissima engine in with its side exhausts necessitating the removal of part of the monocoque that extended alongside the engine. At Spa chronic bearing problems retired the McLaren before practice was finished. With these doctored, the car finished sixth in the British Grand Prix at Brands Hatch to earn Bruce his first Championship point in his own car, but he was really only filling in time and using the Serenissima to develop the chassis while work progressed on the Ford engine in America. The Ford re-appeared for the U.S. Grand Prix at Watkins Glen where Bruce finished fifth, but when it blew during the race in Mexico a final curtain was drawn over the unhappy saga of the first Ford in Grand Prix racing . . .

While the McLaren team wrestled with the overweight underpowered Ford and all its problems, Jack Brabham had taken the aluminium Oldsmobile engine to Repco Engineering in Australia and convinced them that their engineering work to convert the Oldsmobile into an overhead camshaft Formula 1 3-litre engine would be more than made worthwhile by international prestige and publicity for Repco when the Brabhams won races. Jack had to call his cars Repco-Brabhams, but his gamble paid off. In 1966 the Repco gave around 290bhp, when

Jack won the world title, and in 1967 when Denis Hulme won
the Championship in a Brabham he had around 330bhp – the
figure the McLaren team had been working for in the winter of
1965.

In 1967 Ford of Britain announced that they had financed
Cosworth Engineering to the tune of £100,000 to build in
addition to the 1.6 litre engine for Formula 2, a 3-litre Ford V8
engine for Formula 1. Fitted exclusively in the works Lotus 49s
that season the engine won first time out at Zandvoort with Jim
Clark driving, and the Ford-engined Lotus won the British,
U.S. and Mexican Grands Prix during the first season. In 1968
the Ford-Cosworth DFV V8 was made available to other
teams, including McLaren Racing, and it became the power
unit that dominated Formula 1 until Ferrari found form with
their flat-12 in 1970.

Keith Duckworth, the designer of the Cosworth engines,
defined the requirements of a racing engine writing in the
authoritative annual *Autocourse* in 1966 while he was still working on the design of the Formula 1 V8:

'The primary function of a racing engine is to propel the car
in which it is fitted across the finishing line ahead of all the other
cars. The function of the racing engine designer is to produce an
engine which has the best combination of power, weight, size,
accessibility and fuel consumption. The power must be usable
over an adequate range, the weight must be as low as is consistent with reliability and the overall lay-out must be well suited
to the general configuration of the car. Accessibility is probably
less important in an engine built for "works" use than in one
which is for sale to customers, but even so such things as the
plugs and the rest of the ignition system should be easy to get at.
Fuel consumption is possibly one of the most important features
of all, for it governs the shape and size of the car and its conse-
quent starting line weight.'

With the Ford-Cosworth engine reserved for Team Lotus in
1967, the McLaren team decided to use the 3-litre BRM V12
which was being developed ostensibly for sports car customers

because the BRM works team were running the complex H-16
engines. Delivery was not expected before mid-season, so a
2.1 litre version of the BRM V8, enlarged from the 1.5 litre V8,
was fitted into one of the pretty little monocoque McLaren M4
Formula 2 cars. This car ran until just after the Dutch Grand
Prix when it was gutted by fire during tyre tests at Goodwood.
Until the BRM V12 engine arrived, Bruce drove one of Dan
Gurney's 12-cylinder Weslake-engined Eagles.

The M5A chassis waited in the workshops until the BRM
V12 engine finally arrived just before the Canadian Grand
Prix and Bruce ran the car until the end of the season but
because of the late delivery of the engine it was very much a
fill-in motorcar as design work progressed on the M7A Formula
1 cars to take the Ford-Cosworth V8 and the team have used
that engine since.

Bruce learned the basics about engines after school in his
father's garage in Auckland and he put this knowledge to
practical use on his Ulster Austin 7, the Ford Ten special that
followed it, his father's much-modified Austin Healey 100–4,
and finally a string of cars with Coventry Climax engines that
started with the bob-tailed 1,500 Cooper sports car he bought
from Jack Brabham in 1957 and ended with the 2.7 litre Climax
engine that was taken out of the Zerex Special in 1964 and replaced with the 3.9 litre Oldsmobile V8.

Bruce had won the 'Driver to Europe' scholarship in 1958
driving a single-seater 1,750cc Cooper-Climax; he won his first
Grand Prix – the U.S. at Sebring in 1959 – in a works 2.5 litre
Cooper-Climax, and he won the Monaco Grand Prix in 1962
with a V8 1.5 litre Cooper-Climax. He had a close working
relationship with Walter Hassan and Harry Spears at Coventry
Climax and when a special 2.7 litre version of the Formula 1
4-cylinder was built for Jack Brabham to use in the Cooper at
Indianapolis in 1961, Bruce was able to use these units on the
Tasman series. He also worked with the Climax engineers on a
short-stroke version of the 2.5 litre FPF engine when the Tasman
series was limited to a maximum of 2.5 litres on pump fuel in

1964. For 1970 the Tasman regulations were opened to allow 5-litre pushrod engines in addition to the 2.5 litre racing engines.

Prices of the Coventry Climax engines in that period and their horsepower figures make interesting reading. In its Mark 2 version in 1960 the 2.5 4-cylinder FPF engine gave 240bhp at 6,500rpm and it cost £1,750. The Mark 2 version of the FPF engine in 1.5 litre form when the formula changed in 1961, gave 150bhp at 7,200rpm and it cost £1,500. The first of the 1.5 litre Climax V8s – the FWMV – gave 180bhp on carburettors at 8,500rpm and it cost £2,500 in 1962, but for 1963 when a short-stroke version of the V8 was developed using fuel injection the horsepower rose to 200bhp at 9,750rpm and the price doubled to £5,000.

When the Ford-Cosworth DFV V8 was first offered for sale in 1968 it was giving 410bhp at 9,000rpm and it cost £7,500.

Bruce was not convinced that there was no substitute for cubic inches when they talked about going sports car racing in 1964, but it soon became apparent after a few races in England with the Zerex that the extra horsepower and torque of the Oldsmobile was badly needed. In fact the 3.9 litre aluminium Oldsmobile weighed little more than the 4-cylinder Climax engine and in Traco trim it gave 300bhp. The Oldsmobile was eventually enlarged to 5-litres with 380bhp during 1965 but Bruce was fighting a losing battle against the Chaparrals with their 6-litre aluminium Chevrolet V8s. These aluminium Chevrolet engines were strictly 'back door' units for Jim Hall's team, and Bruce's only alternative in the horsepower race was to fit a cast iron Chevrolet – something that offended his ideals of a sports car being light, compact and competitive.

In 1966 the team was really hurting for horsepower that the Traco-Oldsmobile patently did not have, and for the St Jovite race in June they fitted a 5.4 litre 480bhp cast iron Chevrolet, and with a bonus of an extra 100 horsepower, Bruce won the race. Why had he stuck to the Oldsmobile for so long? 'I guess we were wrong,' Bruce wrote in *Autosport* after his win in

Canada. 'In the early stages of sports car racing, development of tyres and transmissions hadn't reached the stage where 500bhp could be reliably used. Now it has.'

Bruce was still suffering a 100lb. handicap over the aluminium Chevrolets in the Chaparrals, but he was surprised to be impressed at the performance of these American push-rod passenger-car engines. 'These Chevvy engines are damned good,' he wrote at the end of the 1966 season. 'At 5.4 litres our engines are twice as big as the 2.7 Climaxes we used to use and which were and still are very good engines. The Climax gave about 240bhp with twin overhead camshafts and as much racing experience as could be crammed into it, and yet these Chevvys of ours are giving 480bhp and they are common-or-garden pushrod engines with single camshafts, and you can buy most of it (if you happen to live in the USA) just down the road for a few dollars. They are strong Mothers and we've found them to be pretty reliable. It certainly makes you think twice before down-rating some of this "Detroit Iron".'

The capacity of the Chevrolet was soon increased to 6-litres with stronger connecting rods and a new fuel injection system which put the power up to 527bhp. As Bruce commented, they now had race-winning potential – all they wanted was some race wins. But the wins were not forthcoming and John Surtees won the first CanAm championship in 1966 with his 5-litre Lola T70.

The story was different in 1967. The sophisticated M6A used the 6-litre engine again, modified by Gary Knutson and the cars won five of the six CanAms with Bruce taking the title. For 1968 the long-awaited aluminium 7-litre Chevrolet blocks were made available to the McLaren team for the first time, and they were fitted into the M8A. This was an advanced design that set a CanAm trend with the engine acting as a stressed member of the chassis with the monocoque halting abruptly behind the cockpit. The M8As won four of the six CanAms in 1968 and this time it was Hulme's turn for the title.

An engine building shop had now been set up in the Colnbrook workshops in England to defend the McLaren title as King of CanAm, and when Gary Knutson left to re-join Chaparral, an employee of Traco Engineering George Bolthoff, was hired to take his place.

The team had decided that using engines modified by Traco or Bartz was more expensive than setting up their own engine facility. There was also a problem in that any power modifications discovered by the McLaren team immediately found its way into other customers' engines. 'We felt that it would be better if we did our own engines and used our knowledge solely for our own benefit,' said Teddy Mayer.

There were problems, however, in preparing American engines for an American series of races from a workshop in England. Supply lines were extended so much that delivery became difficult and on occasions almost impossible.

In England it was hard to find a machine shop familiar with American V8 engines or equipped to handle them. 'Even small jobs that you can do easily in the States, you couldn't do at all in England. They had no equipment to handle V8s, whereas in the States the V8 is the average engine and there are a lot of shops that can handle custom work,' says Bolthoff.

So the decision was taken to set up an engine shop for the team in America and a new company, McLaren Engines Incorporated, was formed at the end of 1969 and a factory building was rented in the City of Livonia on the outskirts of Detroit. Detroit was chosen because of its proximity to the engine suppliers and also because it was a central point for the CanAm races on the East Coast and the mid-West, as well as Indianapolis which is a 250-mile, five-hour drive from Detroit. Also there were daily freight flights from London to Detroit and a telex message flashed to the parent factory could have a part on hand in Detroit within twenty-four hours.

Colin Beanland was made general manager of McLaren Engines, while Bolthoff looked after the engine building and race preparation. In one corner of the 4,500 sq. ft. building, they installed a Heenan & Froude dynamometer in a specially built test cell adequately sound-proofed to drown the bellow of a revving CanAm engine to a muffled rumble. Half of the building is given over to space where the CanAm cars are prepared between races, as the Detroit facility is also used as a CanAm base. The Indianapolis cars and engines are also prepared in Detroit.

Bolthoff, at the age of thirty-seven, came into the engine building side of racing through dragsters. He ran a double-A gas dragster with a 392 cu. in. Chrysler V8 stroked and bored to 465 cu. in. and fitted with a 671 supercharger. It ran 197mph, with a 7.97sec E.T. which was a world record for the class which Bolthoff held while he ran professionally from 1963 to 1965. He was working with Traco when he heard through the grapevine that Gary Knutson was leaving the McLaren team, so he telephoned Teddy Mayer in England and applied for the job the instant it became available.

With the strip, check, and re-assemble jobs done on the 4-cylinder turbo-charged Offenhausers for the M15 McLarens at Indianapolis completed, Bolthoff joined Lee Muir and John Nicholson on the build for the 1970 CanAm engines.

When the engines arrive from Chevrolet they are the absolutely bare 430 cu. in. aluminium blocks as sold over the counter or fitted as an option on a Corvette. The other parts are mostly stock from Chevrolet, and they are then modified as necessary. These blocks are treated very much as raw material and they are extensively re-worked. All the dimensions are checked, the blocks are line-bored to ensure accuracy, and the deck surface is machined to true it up. The rough edges of sand casting and aluminium flash are all removed in the process.

'We do the porting work on the stock heads and then we fit special aluminium bronze valve guides that we make in England. The valves are stock. Chevrolet have a high performance valve that's about the best thing you can buy. Wherever possible we stick with standard Chevrolet parts where they work, because there's no sense in trying something tricky that may not work.

'The manifolds and rocker covers are all made in England,

but we do the hand work on them here. We have to port the manifolds, and set up the butterflies and throttle assemblies. The manifolds are McLaren Racing designs, but the fuel injection parts are all from Lucas.

'The main problem with adapting the engine to fit the CanAm car is in the re-routing of the oil system to fit the headers. The headers come down very close to the block and we have to modify the oil inlet lines to get the engine into the car physically.'

The engine is fitted with a dry-sump oil system because the high lateral G load during cornering would interfere with oil pick-up on a normal wet sump engine. Doing away with the standard oil sump also allows the engine to be mounted lower in the chassis.

The 465 cu. in. (7.5 litre) engines use the 430 ZL-1 Corvette aluminium option block fitted with a crankshaft from a 427 cu. in. engine that is standard in the Corvette and other Chevrolet models. This standard crankshaft is nitrided as are the camshafts before they are installed in the racing version of the engine.

'We see about 675bhp from a good 564cu.in. engine. I think in its basic 430cu.in. form as a Corvette option it's rated at about 450bhp or maybe less because Chevrolet are a little conservative about their rated horsepower. On the Corvettes especially. I imagine that if you took a good Corvette and gave it a sharp tuneup you'd get close to 500 horsepower out of it. . . .'

The engine weighs 460lb. in racing trim for its 675 horsepower and Bruce eagerly rated it as a better power unit on a horsepower-per-pound basis than any other racing engine, including the 3-litre 4-cam 32-valve Cosworth V8 Grand Prix engine that weighs 360lb. and gives 430 horsepower. Bruce had invented the weight-to-power ratio for a Reynolds Aluminium news release, but it was still a fact that the aluminium pushrod Chevrolet stacked up better than the pure racing engine.

The engine test cell cost around $30,000 to install with the dynamometer as the most expensive single item at $8,500. In fact the dynamometer itself is a small part of the installation and it needs many accessories. An accurate tachometer is required, an efficient water system with a good supply of water, and a quiet exhaust system. The McLaren installation has a large pair of industrial silencers twelve-feet long and three feet in diameter mounted on the roof.

The dynamometer absorbs engine torque in water wheel effect. Basically the 'dyno' works as a water wheel and the more water you put into it, the more torque it absorbs, and it is controlled by running water in and out of the 'water wheel'. The torque is read out directly on a scale, and then the torque is converted with the rpm figure into horsepower.

Bolthoff explains the dyno procedure with an engine fresh from a rebuild. 'The dyno more or less simulates the installation in the car. You start it and run it until it warms up. With these aluminium engines you have to torque the heads down and set the valves while they are hot – we call this a hot torque and valve set operation. It takes about ten or fifteen minutes before the temperatures get up to 180°F on water and 200°F on the oil. As the temperature rises the block grows about ten thousandths of an inch in all directions which means that all the valve clearances change. If you set the clearances with the engine cold they get way out as the engine warms up, so this is why we have to do the settings with the engine hot.

'We have a 2½-hour run-in cycle. We start out at 2,500rpm with a light load and eventually end up at about 4,500rpm with a fairly heavy load on it. You get the load by adjusting the amount of water inside the dyno. This is done with a hydraulic and electronic control system. When we've got it warmed up and run in, we check it for oil leaks to make sure it isn't going to leak oil in the race car, we take a quick horsepower reading and if it's reasonable we take the engine off and put it in the car.

'If we don't have time to run the engine in on the test bed, we have to do it in the car, but this is difficult. On the dyno, we can walk round the engine while it's running and check for oil leaks, but at the track you can tell that there's an oil leak because the airstream blows it all round the engine it's hard to pinpoint exactly where the leak is.'

Bruce impressed George with his knowledge of the entire system of the car and the engine, and he always took a practical interest in developments. George designed the ram stack adaptor with a curve in the casting allowing the use of a straight pipe which can easily be changed to alter the ram stack length. 'I was going to put the fuel injection nozzle straight in at 90 degrees to the butterfly shaft, but Bruce made the suggestion that if the nozzles were swung round by 45 degrees, the body could be made to fit in much closer to the engine. He could pick up things like this quickly because he saw the car as a whole, and not as separate units joined together.'

Throttle linkages were Bruce's pride and joy, and he used to work for days perfecting a set of linkages for the Weber carburettors on his Tasman Coopers. The linkages on the CanAm engines were Bruce's design. 'That was one of his pet things. We tried to make a super zoomy linkage to the metering unit and I worked for a couple of days on a prototype thing to make it sanitary. I thought it was really nice until Bruce came over and looked at it and started shaking and moving it until he just about broke it off. He didn't like it and that was the end of it. I hadn't given it quite the test he had! Denny is like this too. He bends and twists things and if they give, then he's right. . . .'

Teddy Mayer says there is as much work in building the pushrod Chevrolet into a CanAm engine as there would be in modifying a Chevrolet passenger car to go racing. 'There is so much detail that needs changing or modifying or uprating or updating or checking or blueprinting or servicing, that it gets to be a monumental sort of task. Because the block and heads and crankshaft are available from a production line, those parts are reasonably cheap, but after that the expense is about equal with a Formula 1 engine. Our CanAm engines cost about £5,500 each, compared with a Formula 1 Ford Cosworth at £7,500.'

Per race maintenance costs on the Formula 1 engines works out at about £500 for each engine. The Ford-Cosworth gives 430bhp but this figure is not guaranteed, nor is it average, according to Mayer. 'The horsepower that you race with is whatever comes out after the engines have been rebuilt. Even specialists like Cosworth don't always know why a particular engine gives ten or fifteen or even twenty horsepower more than the engine built alongside it on the bench. They know that an engine with a peculiarly happy set of tolerances and parts and just general circumstances runs better, and they know why it should, but they don't know how the engine happens to be built like that, or often what's involved in the peculiarly happy set of circumstances. Cosworth have had problems with servicing the engines, but this is understandable with seventy engines in service and five major Formula 1 teams using them. Like a race car, an engine responds to being built and cared for by expert mechanics, and the number of expert mechanics available at Cosworth or anyone else, is very limited. So you presume that some of the engines are being built and cared for by people who aren't as good, and like race cars they don't respond as well as if they were "tweaked" by the best.'

Before a season in Grand Prix racing the McLaren team can budget fairly accurately on an engine programme. They know they will need seven engines representing an outlay of $126,000 (£52,500) to be certain of having at least four engines at a race for two cars.

Their engine budget is formidable taken in total. They have four turbocharged Offenhauser Indianapolis engines which cost $25,000 (£10,416) each, and they maintain six CanAm engines which represents a total of $79,200 (£33,000).

This makes an initial outlay for engines to compete in Grand Prix, CanAM and Indianapolis-type racing that totals a staggering $305,200 (£116,748) – or more than Ford of Britain invested in Cosworth Engineering to design and build their world-beating Grand Prix engine!

7 Teddy Mayer as Business Partner and Team Manager

When motor racing changed from its 'bung-ho' amateur standing and gradually switched to being an intensely professional sport, there were those who strongly criticized the commercialism, blissfully unaware or ignorant of the immense costs involved. Why, they argued, does racing have to be big business when it has survived for decades without the emphasis on cash support? It was difficult for the purists to realize that precisely because European racing had gone for years without being businesslike and without emphasizing the amount of trade backing it received, it was necessary to effect a quick means of rescuing major motor racing from going bankrupt. Advertising was allowed on racing cars and sponsors who had supported racing for years were at last able to get some recognition for their support. It also opened the door to sponsors outside motor sport to gain publicity and to provide extra backing for the growing number of teams. In America, of course, racing has always had a commercial bias and the problems that ruffled the feathers of the amateurs in Europe were regarded there as faintly comical.

Bruce McLaren's racing team grew from humble beginnings around Bruce's talent as a racing driver, his reputation as a 'nice guy', and his ability to pick the right people to work with him. Running the Zerex Special with a three-man team, however, was a far simpler operation from a cash and organizational point of view than it was soon to become when the team shifted to larger premises with a higher rent, and employed more mechanics for the McLaren sports car project. At about this critical stage in the team's history towards the end of 1964,

Teddy Mayer joined the company as a director bringing with him a welcome boost to the team's bank balance and the promise of increasing his own by applying his keen mind to the business of motor racing.

Edward Everett Mayer, known as Teddy and sometimes as 'The Weener', had left Cornell with a law degree but his consuming hobby was motor racing and before devoting himself to tax law he decided to work at furthering the career of his young brother Timmy who was showing a Jackie Stewart-like flair as a driver and was soon to precede Stewart into Ken Tyrrell's Formula Junior team, racing in Europe. Ken saw a good future for Timmy, and had he not been killed during practice for the last Tasman race of the 1964 Series he would have driven for the Cooper team as number two to Bruce McLaren that season.

Timmy raced in America with a Formula Junior Cooper and a Cooper Monaco sports car run by his brother Teddy, before he was spotted by Tyrrell and when he went to England in 1963 Teddy accompanied him. 'I went over with Timmy as an observer to try and further his interests in racing, and also to see if there was any possibility of a job in racing for me.'

During 1963, Teddy was given to understand by John Cooper that there was a real chance for him to be employed in some form of team management capacity the following season, but Timmy's death cancelled those plans. To gain experience in single-seaters with comparable power to the then 1.5 litre Formula 1 cars, the Mayers arranged to build a twin Cooper to Bruce's and embark on the 1964 Tasman series as a joint team venture. 'After Timmy was killed I'd gone home and attended to his estate and gone to Vermont ski-ing for two or three weeks to sort myself out and decide what I wanted to do.'

Back in England at this time Bruce was at our rented house in New Malden with Wally Willmott and me, working out what the team should turn its attention to now. Sports car racing looked like being a field offering a chance of success and the decision was taken to buy the Zerex Special from John Mecom with a view to campaigning the car in England. Bruce tele-

phoned Teddy in Vermont and asked him to handle the purchase, and Teddy contacted Roger Penske to agree a price and
then called Tyler Alexander to collect the car and arrange its
shipping to Bruce. This re-connection with motor racing up in
the ski resort probably helped Teddy to make up his mind that
he wanted to go motor racing more than he wanted to be a tax
lawyer, so he drafted a proposal, offering his services to the
small McLaren team in a management capacity. Bruce, at the
time, was confident that his own men could handle the programme they had currently embarked upon and he wrote back
suggesting that Teddy might work in America as a McLaren
agent. 'I replied that I didn't think that was a very suitable
arrangement because I had to become completely involved
fulltime in racing or go back to being a lawyer. Finally we
decided that it would be a reasonable idea for me to join the
team, and I wrote a synopsis of the team potential as I saw it. I
felt there was a possibility of it making some money after about
three years, but I wasn't particularly convinced that it would be
an instant success and I certainly wasn't convinced that it was
an excellent financial investment. I didn't see it as a large loss
either – in other words, it was a purely speculative idea for both
Bruce and myself. Bruce was hedging his bets by remaining with
Cooper, and I was hedging mine by not making a large financial
investment and since I was only twenty-six, I still had the
potential of going back and being a lwayer.'

The Mayer family is a wealthy one living in Scranton, Pa.,
and one of Teddy's uncles, Will Scranton, had been Governor
of the state. Teddy was not, as rumour had it at the time, one of
the MGM Mayers. However, he had some financial leeway in
his decisions on what to do with his career and just as he had
concentrated his efforts on management of a person – his
brother – now he applied those intensive efforts in the management of a project – Bruce McLaren Motor Racing Ltd.

Teddy's approach to racing was strict and direct; he didn't
believe in the casual attitude adopted by most people at that
time in racing in England. If a visitor was in the workshop or in

one of the offices passing the time of day and with no intention
of either buying a car or making a deal that was attractive to
McLaren Racing, Teddy would be very likely to drop strong
hints that the person should go someplace else and waste someone else's time. The old pals network in British racing meant
very little to Teddy, but Bruce was aware of how long it had
taken him to meet and become accepted by the barons in the
racing trade and by all the technicians, and he cringed if
Teddy delivered an oral caning over the telephone when a piece
of equipment was late in delivery. Late deliveries were part of
racing in England, but Teddy was not prepared to accept this
languid mañana approach. If it was a business, he reasoned, it
had to be run on a businesslike basis and if company A could not
deliver on time to our specifications, then we should try company B. Often this worked, but often it did not. Bruce had to
work at defusing his explosive new partner, but at the same
time he was taking note of Teddy's business methods. It was just
his application of those methods that worried Bruce.

‘The points that Bruce taught me first had nothing whatever
to do with racing. He had been on his own and in business as an
operating human being outside the sphere of influence of family
and schools and education longer than I had, and he taught me
first of all how to manage myself with regard to other people; a
certain amount of what it took to get along with the world of
motor racing rather than how to go racing or anything about
the technical aspect of it. From time to time there were clashes
of personality between me and other members of the team, but
Bruce almost never had a personality clash with any other member of the team, except me. Sometimes he should have, and
in his last two years he began to learn how to chew people out
and get angry. On the other hand I was probably more than a
little bit the other way. I'd be all for firing a guy if he'd done
something wrong that I considered was really stupid. I think
we learned from each other that sometimes you have to be a
little tougher and sometimes you have to give way a little. You
must remember that both of us were very young when we started.

Some of the people we were working with in our own company were older than we were, and almost everyone we dealt with in business was considerably older, so it was very difficult and we had to learn lessons as we went along.'

What impressed Teddy was the sheer difficulty of going motor racing properly and overcoming all the problems. He told a simple analogy that Bruce enjoyed because it summed up the urgency of racing. 'If you go down to your friendly Ford dealer and order a white Ford with black upholstery, he'll tell you it will be ready two weeks from Monday, but if he phones you on the Friday before and says sorry but it won't be ready until Tuesday, you say well, that's fine, really, no problem. And you go down on the Tuesday and pay the full price for your Ford. But if we arrive at the other end of the world an hour late – not a day late – for a race, no matter whether we've had problems with a dock strike or an unco-operative customs officer or whatever, we not only don't get paid the full price – we don't get paid at all. In other words, in racing there is *no* excuse.

'I was always impressed by the fact that Bruce never gave up. We got involved in the same amount of problems and scrambles everyone else does in racing, but he was willing to keep plugging away until it was over and done with, or we had accomplished the job one way or another. He taught me that you just don't give up. You keep trying various ways. Sometimes you have to swallow your pride and try ways you really feel you shouldn't, particularly in regard to the political aspect of racing.'

Mayer was more than a smart-aleck Yank lawyer come over to revolutionize racing as he soon proved to the rest of the McLaren team, because he was more than willing to work just as hard as they were. If he did things wrong it was from ignorance, not from carelessness, and he figured ignorance was something lessons and experience would put right. Before he married Sally, he lived with Tyler and Wally and me and on occasions Gary Knutson, or Chris Amon, when we rented an enormous house with an overgrown tennis court and an orchard standing well back from the road in Surbiton. We called it 'The

Castle'. Nobody was keen to share a room with Teddy because of his voracious appetite for reading, and his incredible habit of falling asleep in the middle of a sentence and spending the remainder of the night fast asleep with the light on. He was slightly older than the rest of us and took a rather more serious approach to life – plenty of which was going on all round him at 'The Castle'.

At one party after a Guards Trophy sports car race at Brands Hatch, the invitations had been written in Old English, stressing the knights and faire ladies atmosphere of our castle. To heighten the effect (to the amazement of visitors like A. J. Foyt) we had borrowed a suit of armour dummied up in glassfibre, and a couple of very real swords. The highlight of the evening came when Jimmy Clark dressed himself in the armour, donning the lightweight helmet as well as the breastplate, and Graham Hill did an Errol Flynn, leaning out over the stair-rail and proceeding to smite the luckless Jimmy around the head, unaware that the sword was real and Jimmy's armour wasn't.

In case it should be misconstrued that Bruce had the racing ability and Teddy the cash in the company, it is worth pointing out that Bruce always retained a controlling interest in Bruce McLaren Motor Racing Limited, putting his own money in and also, in effect, providing his services as a driver free. 'We considered Bruce's driving as a fee which would have been earned driving for anyone, and adding that to his contributions, it made our interests in the team quite equal.'

Initial sponsorship came when McLaren Racing signed a contract with Firestone at the end of 1964 for the 1965 season. The contract covered an extensive testing programme in addition to sports car racing, because the American type companies were just discovering that European racing was quite different to the racing that they had been used to at tracks like Indianapolis and Indy rubber was certainly not competitive with tyres fielded by Dunlop who had a monopoly in Grand Prix racing at the time Firestone and Goodyear made their appearance. The alliance suited Firestone because they wanted a way into racing that did not involve a big league team until a competitive tyre had been evolved. They also wanted to start racing in a field where it did not matter if they fared badly to begin with. Bruce's specialized knowledge and regular participation in the Tasman series was ideal, and when Bruce took a pair of Coopers south for himself and Phil Hill to drive in the summer of 1965, the cars were shod with Indy-type Firestones.

Race results, of course, were something less than spectacular or immediate, but the elaborate series of tyre testing with Firestone gave the McLaren team a head start in the technical rubber battle that was about to begin. 'It gave us an insight into the problems of rim size, tyre construction and compound at a time when Dunlop were pretty much telling teams they would run, say, 7-inch rims with their only tyre available. You could perhaps raise pressures two pounds or drop them two, but that was all. The situation became more involved when you had a choice not only of shapes, sizes and compounds, but tyre companies as well. For a while we had an advantage because we had some idea from the testing we had done, what was involved in why tyres worked as they did. This certainly was true in sports car racing, and it might have been true in Formula 1 although we had other problems there which prevented us from pressing any advantage we might have.'

This was a difficult period for the team. It was difficult financially because there was the pressure of expansion and the need for extra capital to cover purchase of equipment, cars and engines, and the hiring of personnel. It was difficult because team successes to date had been modest, and difficult because all concerned were learning the business and feeling their way carefully in a highly competitive world where competitors were loath to offer helpful hints.

During 1965 as the team was becoming established, and looking towards Formula 1 for 1966, Teddy gained four distinct impressions of Bruce – as a man, as a businessman, as a racing driver and as an engineer. 'As a man I'd come to know him quite well, possibly better during this period than in the last two or three years of his life, because we were so busy then. And possibly also because with success you start to build a slightly different image both of yourself and your business.

'I had a lot of respect for Bruce as a man. He had a great deal of patience and he had an enormous amount of confidence. Perhaps the confidence was not always entirely well-founded, but it was unshakeable and this was very useful during some of the difficult times we faced.

'As a businessman, Bruce seemed optimistic. I've always felt that if you have something to sell you may have to work hard to sell it, but it will ultimately be saleable. At this period (1965-6) I didn't really think we had much to sell. It needed quite a lot of money to keep even what we had going. Bruce, on the other hand, didn't seem to have a very good idea of how much money it took to do the job, and he had a fairly optimistic theory of how much we were worth.

'As a driver during this period it was difficult for me to assess him. He was more than sufficiently capable to do the job required in our sports cars, but he was still driving for Cooper and it was difficult to know whether his lack of real success at the time was due to the problem with the cars at Coopers, or whether it was due to his driving talent, or his unwillingness to stick his neck out too far. I think Bruce would stick his neck out if he thought we had a real chance to win, but perhaps sticking your neck out is the wrong thing to say because some race drivers drive as hard as they can whether they're first or third or eighth or twenty-eighth. Some race drivers drive very hard if they're first or second and reasonably hard if they're fourth or fifth, and not hard at all if they're tenth or twelfth. Bruce was one of these. He drove well, damned hard, and, I think hung it out a bit if he thought there was a good chance to win. On the other hand if he was running fifth or sixth he would set a reasonable pace for himself which I sometimes felt was below his limit, and wait to see what would happen.

'By comparison Denny falls into the category of a man who will drive reasonably hard all the time, and very very hard if he thinks there is a chance to win. He will not drive very very hard all the time, as a Stewart or a Rindt or a Clark or a Moss might, but he will drive reasonably hard all the time. Bruce wouldn't do that. This is difficult to say because you never know for sure what is going through a driver's mind and there is no sensible way that a manager can force a driver to tell whether he is driving hard. I've heard that it has been done by the Italians and by Neubauer, but it's never been my position with Bruce or with Denny to tell them how hard to drive or to tell them when they're not driving hard enough. I would only have upset them by chipping in my advice. Bruce and Denny had plenty of experience and they knew the score, but this could change with younger drivers and with Peter Revson and Peter Gethin I've tried to apply a little drive psychology and talk them into going steady or giving an all-out effort as the conditions seemed to warrant.

'At the time Bruce knew so much more about the engineering of racing cars than I did that it was difficult to know how good an engineer he was. I got the impression that he had quite a lot of practical experience but he was still learning a good deal of theoretical knowledge, and his testing for Firestone and Ford with their Le Mans cars, plus his wide reading of all the engineering journals he could get his hands on, was adding considerably to his knowledge.'

As team manager in both racing and business, Teddy had some reason for his concern at the financial position. It was not a question of making more money to salt away in the company's coffers; it was a matter of gathering finance to survive. Teddy felt it was probably financial considerations that prompted them to decide on the 4-cam Indianapolis Ford engine that spelt doom to their first Formula 1 season in 1966. 'I have a nasty feeling that if I had not urged the Ford engine more on financial than engineering grounds, Bruce would very probably have found some other solution to our engine problem, and it certainly couldn't have been worse than the one we actually chose.'

When commercialism arrived in motor racing the cries of disgust from the purists came from those angered at the thought that the teams were earning too much money. Probably the owners of small businesses in the process of expansion, were better able to sympathize with the need for extra finance, than were the voluble fans with no direct interest in the racing field.

Mayer feels most teams are in shaky financial positions most of the time if their only interests are in going racing, as opposed to teams backed by a line of production cars (Lotus, Ferrari) or an engineering combine like BRM or Matra. 'The major reasons are that you can have large losses through accidents, either through crashes or blow ups, at any time and these losses are probably of greater magnitude relative to the financial resources of the company, than most businesses would normally hazard. Secondly, I think the whole racing business is peculiarly vulnerable financially. By this I mean racing in itself. Participating in racing alone in no way supports a first-class racing effort. There's just not enough starting money or prize money to begin to support a proper team, therefore you're dependent on sponsorship, and sponsorship is dependent on the financial climate of the time, and upon the success of the team involved. So if for any reason you're unsuccessful or the financial climate is not good, the sponsorship could dry up very quickly.'

Working with Bruce in any sort of management capacity was like standing by a brake ready to apply it if he looked like shooting off at great speed in any direction in pursuit of a new project. Some drivers employ managers to blame when things go wrong, but Bruce was prepared to temper his enthusiasm in the light of other opinions that he respected. Or at least listened to. To eavesdrop on a discussion on future plans or a new car between Bruce, Teddy, Tyler and the designers or mechanics directly concerned, was like overhearing a family fight as the guidelines were established. Bruce would make a point and if it was thought to be without basis or foundation it would be argued down by Teddy or Tyler and Bruce would put the point another way. What sounded like fierce arguments interspersed

with hoots of laughter, always ended with concrete and forward
thinking plans and schedules being made. This 'family' descrip-
tion occurs frequently, in marked contrast to other teams where
the one man's word is law.

'Bruce rarely, certainly more rarely than the converse was
true, tried to impose his thought processes on me. Generally
speaking our votes were equal and we would thrash it out and
come to a decision that we both thought was pretty sensible but
at no time did he throw his weight round with me. The one guy
in the outfit neither of us really managed to convince if he
didn't want to be convinced was Tyler. If he believes he is right
and you're wrong, he'll let you know until it's all over, and
possibly for several years thereafter. . . .'

Phil Kerr joined the company after leaving Jack Brabham
where he had helped to build up a small empire in the eight
years he had been there, and became joint managing director
with Teddy. Prior to Bruce's death Phil handled most of the
administrative work. He would be in on policy decisions but
generally speaking he never cast a vote. 'By the time Bruce and I
had thrashed it out none of us really cast votes because it had
become obvious what to do. Since Bruce's accident Phil's role
has changed somewhat in that on policy we now work fairly
equally. We decide on how we're going to proceed on the basis
of his and my information and thoughts, as opposed to Bruce's
and mine.

'I butted into the technical procedure sometimes more than
Bruce really liked because I was interested in it and because I
felt that I would be able to do a better job with the operational
procedure if I knew what was happening technically. Usually I
would set out the procedure as to how we would accomplish
what we wanted to do, then Bruce and I would discuss it, and in
many cases I would set out both the technical and operational
procedure. This wasn't because I was qualified to do so, but I
liked setting out procedures, and Bruce was often busy on other
jobs and didn't particularly like the job of putting things down
on paper. Although he generally left operational procedures

largely to me, he would correct my technical procedures a great deal and then he would proceed with the technical side and I would execute the operational procedure. It worked out very well. My role has changed somewhat since Bruce's death in that I've had to do his job in setting out the technical procedure purely because it has to be done by someone. Tyler is learning to do a good job in this area, but much of the time he is away with the Formula 1 or CanAm teams. Now I go into the design office as Bruce used to do and say we'll run 12-inch discs and a wing on the top and a radiator out the back, because someone has to say "That's what we've got to do". The designers will do a better job than any of us – than Bruce could have done, or I could certainly have done – but they want help in saying "That's it".'

Teddy carries his air of clinical business correctness to the track with specially printed McLaren Racing timing charts to record not only every lap time but every driver comment during pit stops, and every alteration made to the car. He carries his watches, his yellow foolscap legal pads, and his charts and Gold Cross pens to the pits in an expensive tan leather briefcase with a combination lock. An interesting tale surrounds the first time Teddy set the combination on his new briefcase and promptly forgot it . . .

During these long test days at Goodwood, sorting out new cars or refining current machinery, Teddy learned a lot about what is required from a driver in evaluating racing cars. He classes Bruce and Denny in different categories, both achieving results, but these results being gained by different means.

'I've given a good deal of thought to Bruce's ability as a car-sorter and development driver. This was tremendously important to the company, and intellectually it was of tremendous interest to me. Bruce worked very hard at being a development driver but I don't think that he was always entirely unbiased if he had a pet theory he wanted to prove. He was generally better at telling you *how* to fix a problem than he was at deciphering whether or not the problem had been fixed. For

1 Bruce McLaren in the Ulster Austin Seven that taught him the rudiments of racing and engineering, seen here at a sprint meeting in New Zealand when Bruce was sixteen.

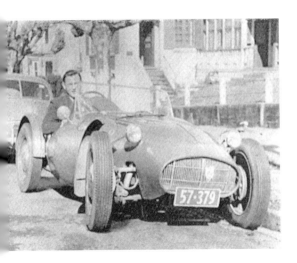

2 The Ulster Austin was replaced by this Ford Ten special which Bruce drove to school and competed in occasionally, but never really liked.

3 Bruce's first 'real' racing car was the ex-Brabham bob-tailed 1500 Cooper sports car that he raced during the 1957 season in New Zealand.

4 Bruce with his father, mother, and sister Janice at their home in
Uplands Road, Remuera, after his first season racing overseas.

5 Bruce McLaren in the 1,750cc Cooper heads Ross Jensen in the 250F
Maserati, Ron Roycroft (Ferrari 4.5), Bib Stillwell (Cooper 1.5), Ron
Frost (Cooper 1.5) another 250F Maserati and a P3 Alfa Romeo at
Ardmore in the first heat of the 1958 Grand Prix.

6 Colin Beanland and Bruce work in the McLaren garage at Remuera preparing the 2-litre Cooper for the New Zealand races in 1959 when Bruce won the national championship.

7 The 1959 Cooper Grand Prix team: Jack Brabham, Masten Gregory, and Bruce McLaren.

8 Bruce on his way to winning the 1964 Tasman Championship in the slimline 2.5 litre Cooper.

9 Bruce and Timmy Mayer discussing a handling problem with one of the 2.5 litre slimline Tasman Coopers at Pukekohe in 1964.

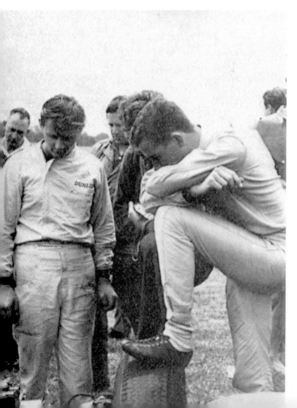

10 Battered and bloody from the flying stones at Rheims in the 1959 French Grand Prix, Bruce is helped from his Formula 1 Cooper by Ken Tyrrell.

11 Saloon racing was a branch of the sport that Bruce McLaren never really liked. Here he spins Peter Berry's 3.8 Jaguar at Brands Hatch in 1961 amid the Jaguars of Graham Hill (leading), Mike Parkes and Roy Salvadori.

12 'The Jolly Green Giant' in all its glory in the overcrowded workshop's space in New Malden. This shot was taken just after the Zerex chassis had been replaced and the 4-cylinder Coventry Climax engine had been swapped for the Oldsmobile V8. Vertical exhaust stacks were fitted because there was no time to make proper manifolds before the first race!

13 The Zerex was rushed across to Canada for the Mosport race in June 1964 which Bruce won. The car was re-christened the Cooper-Oldsmobile.

14 Last minute McLaren conference at Brands Hatch where Bruce won the Guards Trophy in the Cooper-Oldsmobile as the Zerex was then known. Eoin Young, Wally Willmott and Bruce Harre (left) and the Americans Tyler Alexander and Teddy Mayer consulting their Rolexes.

15 Jim Clark and Bruce were always good friends. In Lotus Grand Prix cars Jim was top, but Bruce could beat him when it came to pitting the McLaren sports cars against the Lotus.

16 The crew of the salvage truck had to strip to rescue Bruce's 1965 Tasman Cooper from a water-filled ditch at Pukekohe when he spun on oil during a pre-race heat. He was unhurt but a rear wheel was torn off.

17 Bruce, in front, heading down to the Station Hairpin at Monaco in 1965 with the works Cooper. Behind him is Richard Attwood in a Lotus.

18 Bruce believed in hiring New Zealanders on his team. With the Mallite chassis of the first McLaren Formula 1 car in 1966 are, from left: Eoin Young, Howden Ganley, Bruce McLaren, Bruce Harre, Colin Beanland, Chris Amon, and John Muller.

19 Robin Herd left an advanced design career in the aircraft industry to join the McLaren team in 1965. He left in 1969 to work for Cosworth Engineering and is now designer of the March cars.

20 Bruce McLaren had the ability to relax and sleep anywhere at any time – even just before a race!

21 Bruce McLaren and Chris Amon on the front row of the grid in the Labatt 50 race at Ste Jovite in 1966. Wally Willmott and Tyler Alexander wait beside Bruce's car while Bruce Harre and Colin Beanland talk with Chris.

22 One of Denny Hulme's less conventional winning finishes was at Mosport in 1967 when he went off the road two laps from the finish and broken bodywork slashed the left front tyre. He limped to the finish pouring smoke from the damaged tyre and won the race!

23 McLaren CanAm formation at Riverside in 1968 with the M8A. Bruce won the race and Denny Hulme was fifth.

24 Bruce in the winged McLaren M7 at Monaco in 1968 during practice. He spun on oil in the tunnel and crashed on the first lap of the race!

25 After Bruce's death in 1970, Peter Gethin, who had driven
McLarens to win the 1969 and later the 1970 Formula 5000
championships, was signed to drive the works McLarens in Grand Prix
and CanAm races. Peter is seen here with his team leader Denny
Hulme in the McLaren M14A.

26 Team talk in the pits at Brands Hatch, watched by Phil Kerr, joint
managing director of the McLaren company. These McLaren/Hulme
tactic talks with Denny sprawled across the nose of Bruce's car were
an informal feature of the McLaren team.

27 The wedge-shaped M16 McLaren built for the 1971 Indianapolis 500.

28 The ram stacks for the fuel injection on the McLaren-built CanAm Chevrolet engines.

29 Bruce McLaren,
Tyler Alexander,
Teddy Mayer and
Phil Kerr.

30 Bruce
McLaren, with
his wife Patty
and daughter
Amanda.

31 One of Bruce's
favourite projects was
this GT version of the
M6 CanAm sports car
seen outside his front
door at Burwood
Park. Bruce used the
M6GT as a road car
to evaluate the
chances of building a
production version.

32 Bruce at Goodwood in May 1970 testing Denny Hulme's new M8D
sports car. Bruce's fatal accident occurred while he was testing his own
M8D on June 2.

33 In 1966 Bruce took Michael Cooper with him in the new M6A
CanAm sports car while it was being tested at Goodwood and this
photograph of Cooper's shows the driver's eye view of the straight with
the marshal's post on the right which Bruce hit in his fatal crash
during CanAm testing in 1970.

example, if you put a different rear tyre on and sent Bruce out, he might do fifty laps and come in to say he thought it was better or thought it was worse. If you put the same tyre on Denny's car he could come in after ten laps and say the tyre was either better or it was worse and he would eventually be proved right. Ultimately Bruce would end up where Denny had ended up, but Denny would never have any idea *why*, whereas Bruce would have a good idea of what was causing the problem, or what the characteristics were. Denny would just know that it was worse or better.

'Really if you were going to a race track to race rather than test, Denny is a better sorter than Bruce was. Denny will arrive at a reasonably quick solution to the car faster than Bruce, but if you were going testing with a car that was miles out of the ballpark, Bruce would tell you what was wrong with it and how to fix it. Denny would only know that it was wrong. So obviously for the original sorting-out of the car Denny was not as valuable as Bruce.

'If you tried one thing at a time with Denny – as with most drivers – you would eventually arrive at a solution, but with Bruce you could get there a lot faster because he could sort problems caused by aerodynamics from problems caused by spring rates, from problems caused by tyre size, better than Denny. It's very easy for a driver to be misled here. It's an enormously complicated problem with endless permutations and Bruce was misled any number of times, but he was very good at sorting out the problems and I think he arrived at reasonable solutions very often.'

It took probably a year for the McLaren–Mayer combination to start operating efficiently, and it became obvious that even if Teddy's business methods were a little too super-efficient for England, they were very well suited to negotiations with American companies where the team looked for support and sponsorship. Their main field was sports car racing in the United States so it seemed logical to look to the relatively untapped sponsorship market in the U.S. rather than trying to plead a case with the traditional sponsors in England who were already well committed and not as interested in American racing anyway. From this logic came the Firestone contract (and later the Goodyear contract), a deal with Ford in Detroit to build the GTX which was a special open version of the GT40 built at McLaren Racing in Feltham, and sponsorship with the Gulf Oil Corporation at Pittsburgh, Pa., and the Reynolds Aluminium at Richmond, Va.

Bruce was a very important figure in these contractural discussions for while Teddy talked dollars and cents, Bruce was charming the company principals. But it was not a case of turning this charm on. It was there all the time. The friendly McLaren grin at almost any hour of the day or night could prompt mechanics to keep working, or it could just as easily impress a vice-president by the man's obvious sincerity and the fact that the charm was not false.

'Bruce had a particularly fortunate personality and people liked him immediately. He was adept socially and he made a very good impression on everyone. As a racing driver and therefore in a sense the romantic hero of the team as well as the name which the company sported, Bruce was extremely important in negotiations for sponsorship. Everyone wants to know the principal of the act, and if the act is motor racing then the drivers have the star roles. Businessmen and engineers and mechanics may be very important and the sponsors may want to know who they are and what kind of people they are, but I think they get a bigger kick out of knowing and meeting and talking to the star. Bruce's personality was excellent in this regard and he did an extremely good job just by being himself.'

Teddy believed in getting everything down on paper professionally and it was not unusual after protracted meetings and then a long dinner for Bruce to go to bed and for Teddy to tap away on his little travelling Olivetti using the Hunter method of typing – finding one key and hunting for the next – until he had prepared a complete proposal based on the day's talks. This efficiency could not fail to impress.

As a company director, Teddy was an office tyrant, demanding that desks be spotless and uncluttered by surplus books, papers or pens. He would stomp off muttering about untidy desks and untidy minds. Because he has a very nasal way of speaking it is not always easy for people to understand Teddy when they first meet him, and he would rage at telephone operators who were doing their best. If a telephonist lasted a week in the downstairs switchboard/reception office, she could reckon herself hired. Secretaries had to type faultless letters because Teddy insisted that clean, accurate well-typed letters were good advertisements for the team. The same went for efficient operating of the telephone switchboard. He carried the same necessity for neatness out on to the workshop floor, often grabbing a broom if he couldn't see the cleaner, and sweeping away the offending litter himself.

Teddy's willingness to do the work himself finally won him grudging favour with the mechanics, who were impressed that 'the little grey-haired guy' would be in all day Sunday helping to crate up spares for shipment, and still be there working on schedules in his office when they were going home. In this respect he was like Bruce and both Patty and Sally counted themselves lucky if their men were home for dinner before eight o'clock most nights. Sunday was just another day at the shop if there was a project nearing completion or a freight flight to catch.

Most Americans, as Teddy often observes, like living in America and this was one of the reasons why McLaren Engines Incorporated was set up in Detroit so that they could hire and keep the top American engine men, who were often keen to get home after a few weeks in England. After some vague grumbling about Englishmen who use their baths to keep coal in, and the difficulty of finding a house with a shower or a large U.S. style refrigerator, Teddy settled down to the English way of living. He and Sally and their children Timmy and Anne live in a large country house in the 'stockbroker belt' just outside Esher in

Surrey, about half an hour by 250SE Mercedes or MGB GT to the McLaren shop at Colnbrook. It takes the same time to get to London's Heathrow airport which is important because Teddy spends much of his time in trans-Atlantic commuting or flying to races in Europe.

8 Team driver, Denis Hulme

The little drops coursing down the side of the windscreen on the 1970 Indianapolis McLaren were whipped by the 200mph airstream as Denny Hulme rocketed up to the braking area for Turn 3. He noticed the tiny rivulets and remembered them like the condensation streaming across the windows as a big jet comes in to land. It never occurred to him in that split instant that the drops were methanol fuel leaking from a breather cap that had popped open.

When he got on the brakes, the fuel gushed forwards from the open tank breather just ahead of the cockpit on the left and the wind fanned the spray back over the car on to the red-hot turbocharger behind the Offenhauser engine. The car exploded into a shimmering blast of heat. Denny Hulme had only seconds to escape and the car was still travelling at 180mph. With every second the car was covering 264 feet. He knew there was fuel on the rear tyres and as he braked hard he was prepared for a spin. But the harder he braked the more fuel surged out of the breather to fan the raging clear flames. He feared an explosion, but he was going too fast to jump.

The car was slowing but his hands were already burning. The leather of his gloves had shrunk, turning his fingers into painful claws as he battled with the buckle of his seat harness. The fire extinguisher had exploded but it couldn't cope with the blaze at that speed. It registered as a brief discolouration of the air and it was gone. Wasted. The blast-furnace heat had welded the clear vizor to his Bell Star helmet. His flame proof overalls were starting to char. With the pain of his hands more than he could bear he was wriggling from under the specially-flattened leather-rim steering wheel and trying to stand in the seat. The speed was down to about 70mph and it seemed like a crawl. He turned backwards in the seat and pushed himself out over the rear wheel with his forearm against the roll hoop. His burning hands were useless. He hit the road backwards and bounced, amazingly without breaking any bones. He picked himself up still with the strength to curse the fire crew on the truck that was chasing the runaway burning car. They had not realized that the driver was also on fire.

Denis Clive Hulme is a strong brave man. His father, Clive, had bred this family courage, and for heroism in World War Two he had been awarded the Victoria Cross.

Sitting up in hospital in Indianapolis, coming and going with the pain-stilling drugs, his hands, feet and left forearm caked in white tacky dressing like icing, Denny was still able to chat and titter when Bruce and others in the team called to see him each day. The burns were extremely serious and there was the unspoken chance that he would lose some fingers on his left hand. Bruce was terribly concerned at his condition, their closeness in times of trouble showing through as clearly as it had when they travelled together between races like a couple of kids out on a treat.

When Bruce was killed at Goodwood three weeks later, Denny, who had withstood the pain of his burns without a tear broke down in his grief.

The close relationship between Denny and Bruce grew from mutual respect of the other's ability – Bruce as the engineer and Denny as the driver.

New Zealand is a country of 103,000 square miles with a population of under three million, some 1,200 miles east of Australia in the South Pacific. This comparative isolation from the world breeds parochialism and fierce independent qualities which, when added to an inborn desire to succeed, has resulted in single-minded successful men like Bruce McLaren and Denny Hulme. You could compare the country in area with England; in size of population with Paris. New Zealanders at home tend to be complacent, their complacency assured by their geographical remoteness from world troubles. New Zealanders who make their way in the outside world switch this complacency for compensatory agressiveness that appears in different forms. With Bruce McLaren it was a restless urge to do things better, to develop better racing cars, to rage at indecision. With Denny Hulme it is an almost animal strength, a dogged desire to win, and a blank inability to suffer crowds, boring company, or questioning pressmen.

But such a thumbnail sketch of Hulme as a man with the physique and mentality of an ox does not come close to a true portrait. Behind the craggy façade the reason is probably a basic shyness which is strenuously disguised. The year he won the World Championship on the Grand Prix tracks, the thing that bothered him most about the glory was the round of speeches and public functions he had to attend. That was in 1967. Today Denis copes a little better with his business as a professional racing driver, helped probably by the fact that in 1968 he started driving full-time for the McLaren team and some of the McLaren charm rubbed off. Not a lot, but some.

Some racing drivers are born. Others are made. Denis Hulme was hewn. He was born on June 18, 1936, on a small dairy farm in the tobacco growing area of Motueka at the top of the South Island. His father was invalided out of the army after action in Greece and Crete in 1941, and he came back to New Zealand to buy a small trucking business in the tiny village of Pongakawa, only a mile from the sea and the Bay of Plenty beaches, and a few miles from Te Puke, a slightly larger township with a population of 2,500 people. So there was no excuse for Denny to be any other way than the way he is. He grew up in bare feet, sunshine and sea and spent his spare moments in his father's trucking workshops. After a couple of years in secondary school, Denis left to work for his father. Clive Hulme tells a workshop story of noticing a strange smell and drawing Denny out from under his welding goggles to ask him what it was. It turned out that Denny had stepped on a glowing welding spark that was burning the sole of his bare foot and he had not noticed it!

He was nineteen and earning some extra cash by ferrying new cars down from Auckland to Tauranga for the local Morris dealer when he drove his first sports car. It was a brand new 1,500cc MG TF and even at running-in speeds, Denny was entranced. From then on, the beach took second place to cars. He was working so hard for his father, driving one of the trucks and looking after servicing as well that his father decided to give his son a surprise and bought him a new MG TF. In fact, Denny was probably more taken with the idea of top-down motoring than any thoughts of racing, but he was soon lured into the local car club. In those days anyone with a car that remotely resembled a sporting vehicle was badgered into competing. At his first hillclimb he knocked six seconds off the class record. The bug bit, and in 1958 he moved up to a MGA. The local papers carried reports early in the New Year that a young Aucklander, Bruce McLaren, was going to Europe to race Coopers during the 1958 season, but this meant little more to Denny than the fact that he had seen Bruce and talked with his father on a rally where Denis was driving his MG TF and the McLarens were in their Ford V8 Pilot.

His reputation as a production sports car driver grew and he saw no reason why he should not try a single-seater. By now he knew about Bruce McLaren and the other 'real' racing people and after the Grand Prix at Ardmore in 1959 he bought a 2-litre Cooper-Climax. Denny's habit of driving in bare feet probably stemmed from the balmy club days when they lay about in a pair of shorts and often as not drove just like that when it came to their turn. With the Cooper he earned his 'Driver to Europe' award and in 1960 he and George Lawton (who had equalled Hulme's form in a 2-litre Cooper) were bound for England with their manager/mechanic Feo Stanton. Feo met Denny when they were both driving Hulme gravel lorries.

It was a season of mixed fortunes and tragedy when George was killed on the Roskilde track in Denmark. Denny had raced a Formula 2 Cooper, a Formula Junior Cooper, with one drive at a non-championship Formula 1 race at Snetterton in a 2½-

litre Cooper. He won at Salerno and Pescara in the Formula
Junior car, but these victories seemed unimportant to the New
Zealand public who were reading about Bruce McLaren win-
ning Grand Prix races and finishing second to Brabham in the
World championship.

The first meeting between McLaren and Hulme came about
after the 1960 Grand Prix at Ardmore when Bruce had con-
gratulated the winners of the 'Driver to Europe' award. Denis
took him at his word and called on him as soon as they arrived
in England and Bruce loaned him his Morris Minor while he
shopped for a car of his own. From time to time Bruce would
check on Hulme's progress in among the jigs and trestles and
chassis frames in the dim Cooper workshops. Denny was competing very much in the lower ranks of racing, but, looking
back, he is still able to assess Bruce's ability in Formula 1.

'I thought he was very good, although in a funny way you
could compare him with Fittipaldi stepping into the Lotus 72.
A very good car and a guy coming up with some good races
behind him and winning a Grand Prix very early on. Jochen
Rindt didn't do this. Chris certainly hasn't, and there are others
who have really had to thrash along before they finally succeeded. So maybe he was a little lucky. Without a doubt he was
stepping into the best car around at the time. It was reliable and
quick and he had Jack to guide him. He only came over in 1958
and yet he was second in the World championship in 1960.
That was pretty good.'

At the end of the 1960 season, Denny did a deal with Reg
Parnell to hire a $2\frac{1}{2}$-litre Cooper for the races in New Zealand
during the January of 1961 and with this car he went home and
won the National Gold Star as McLaren had done after his first
season abroad.

It was Denny's inability to cope with the prevailing necessity
to chat people up – the 'old boy' syndrome – that probably kept
him out of the Formula 1 drive in 1961. Denny reasoned that
driving prowess should get you to the top, but he was ignoring
the fact that diplomacy was usually necessary to get the

opportunity to display the prowess in the first place. Denny had a 'foot in the door' with his scholarship award and the publicity that went with it in 1960, but in 1961 on his own it was a different matter. It was uphill all the way.

He bought a Formula Junior Cooper but with a misguided sense of economy he fitted it with a Martin-tuned Ford engine. It was cheaper than other power units but that year it was also less powerful and less reliable. With a tired Mark 1 Ford Zodiac as a tow car he hauled the Cooper round the crowded calendar of European races from Karlskoga in Sweden south to Messina in Sicily.

I travelled with him that summer as someone to talk to, rather than someone to help. Looking back ten years at one of current racing's top money earners, is enlightening and just a little exhausting.

Denny built the Cooper at the factory and his first continental race was the Danish Roskildering. He was travelling with the 1961 'Driver to Europe', Angus Hyslop, who was racing a Lotus 20. Angus won the race and Denny was an also-ran with a fire in his undertray. After the trip down to Rouen in France both cars retired, and a week later the two Kiwis were to drive a Fiat Abarth 850 in the Le Mans 24-hour race. We stayed at a small hotel in the country outside Le Mans while Denny did an engine rebuild on the footpath outside, throwing a cover over the car and coming in for a beer when it rained. They ran without a clutch to win their class and place fourteenth overall. From Le Mans we headed south to Caserta in the middle of Italy where Denny started on pole but dropped back with a bent gear selector.

Up to Monza in the royal park outside Milan a fortnight later, book in at the hotel, unload the race car at the track, and discover that Hulme's entry has not been received. Some terse comments from Hulme who was trying to remember if in fact he had sent it in, and then an all-night drive over the Alps through Switzerland to Rheims where a race was being held the same weekend. He finished seventh and then headed back to England for a refit.

If Formula Junior racing qualified as a circus, the Hulme entourage certainly smacked of a gypsy caravan. The Zodiac was as purchased with a vase of plastic flowers that had never been tossed away for some reason, a defunct rev counter, a row of extra instruments that all read either zero or 212, and a siren which had a miraculous effect in clearing traffic in European villages. This siren almost resulted in Hulme's equipe being reduced to ashes in France when the overloaded electrical system went up in smoke. Denis, resourceful as ever, quelled the blaze by pulling out the fuses – half a screwdriver and a drill bit! The rear seats were removed and the back of the car and the boot were crammed with spare parts and petrol cans. Standard practice was to fuel the racing car after each event as well as the six spare five-gallon cans, and this was usually enough to keep the Zodiac fuelled as far as the next track. His headquarters in England was the Lamb Inn at Kingston, a pub where the Scarab crew were also staying during their fruitless assault on the Grand Prix racing that year.

The next race was at Messina in Sicily and we set off in convoy with Hyslop's team on a Tuesday morning. 112 hours and 1,800 miles later we were crossing on the ferry to Sicily. Angus won the race and Denis came second. 'We couldn't have planned it better with a shotgun', remarked Hyslop's mechanic, Bill Hannah.

That winter Denis stayed in England and worked in one of the Jack Brabham garages, planning to update his Cooper and race it again in 1962. It was a dismal year for him, making 1961 look like a good time. Brabham's manager, Phil Kerr could see the potential in Denny, but Jack was not at all convinced. It took an accident which broke the collarbone of the 'works' Formula Junior driver to get Denny into a factory Formula Junior Brabham for the first time at the end of the 1962 season and he proved his point. In 1963 he was armed with a works Brabham and in fourteen starts he brought home seven wins and four second places.

For 1964 he had a works Formula 2 Brabham, and in 1965 he

was being given occasional Formula 1 drives. In 1966 he was partnering Jack in the Grand Prix team. At Le Mans, co-driving a Ford GT40 with Ken Miles, he finished second to the McLaren/Amon Ford in the fouled-up 'photo finish'.

Jack won the World championship in 1966 and Denny won it in 1967. He was also 'Rookie of the Year' when he finished fourth at Indianapolis in an Eagle, and in an M6A McLaren sports car he won three of the six races on the 1967 CanAm trail, finished second to Bruce in the championship and won $40,000.

For 1968, however, he decided to leave Jack and join the McLaren team. Denny acknowledged the fact that the Brabham team had given him his chance to make a name in racing, but Jack was well aware that Denny had outgrown his 'number two' slot, and there wasn't really room for another driver who wanted to win – especially if it involved beating the boss to do it!

With the McLaren team Denny settled down quickly to an established routine. Bruce was the sorter-outer and the engineer and he was quick in CanAm cars. Denny was quick anyway, but it was recognized that he was faster than Bruce in Formula 1.

'Bruce was quicker than me in CanAm,' says Denny, 'and I sort of knew that he was going to be quicker as well. He would set his car up the way he wanted it and he was very smooth. He liked CanAm racing. It was his one big thing and it made the world of difference. He was the hardest guy to beat in a CanAm car and yet he could put the same amount of effort into a Grand Prix car and get nothing like the same results. I think one of the reasons for this was that he was so smooth. If you throw a CanAm car around you lose time, whereas the only way to get a Grand Prix car to go quick is to start hurling it round and really get it set up for fast corners. I don't think Bruce liked doing this somehow'.

Other differences came in their acceptance of people. 'Bruce used to like going out and meeting people. He managed to cope even when they were asking the most ridiculous questions whereas my natural reaction was to think "what a bunch of idiots we've got here", and either tell them so or not talk to them at all. But that's just the way I am. Bruce could spend the whole night entertaining people and this is how he made lots of friends. He was the same with the Press. He always had time to talk with them. I've never been able to do this. For certain people in the Press, yes, but for most of them, no. There's probably only half a dozen I can sit and talk to, but the rest of them . . . I feel they should do their homework more and find out what it's all about . . . Bruce always coped with them better.'

Bruce said that Denny was one of the talent-spotter Ken Tyrrell's rare mistakes. Ken never reckoned that Denny would make the grade, but Bruce also acknowledged Ken's covering maxim that a good 'hungry' driver would always beat a good 'fat' one. For someone who looked like 'missing the boat', Hulme has not done badly. Since he started Formula 1 racing seriously with a regular works driver in 1966, Denny has been fourth, first, third, sixth and fourth in the World championship, and has won five Grands Prix.

In hospital in 1970 Denny was telling everyone that he would be driving the CanAm car at Mosport in mid-June less than a month away. 'The doctors just sort of laughed about it. I think they thought I was being a bit optimistic . . .'

A week before the race he could not bend either of his hands, but with typical Hulme homespun therapy he was wandering about the McLaren workshops with a steering wheel forcing his fingers to close round the rim. He finished third in that first CanAm race with hands raw under the bandages where blisters had burst. But to Denny that race was a gesture. He had set his heart on Mosport to bolster his own spirits during the painful days in hospital, but eventually he was aiming at Mosport with grim determination to 'do it for Bruce'. In several of his early races he had to bend the fingers of his left hand round the steering wheel and trap it there for the race, doing all the work with his right hand.

The left hand, shiny with scar tissues, still lags behind the recovery of the right hand and he favours it when handling a fork or dressing. At one stage he had to be careful even when reading the newspaper because the sharp edge of the page could slice his tender hands.

Once a racing driver had to concentrate on keeping fit, but now he seldom has time. Apart from the occasional swim in the motel pool after a race, Denny says the work-out involved in driving the cars and getting from race to race keeps him in trim. 'It's difficult to say how fit you've got to be. You don't have to front up and run a four-minute mile – it's more important to be able to pace yourself, to know your own capacity and to make it last the race. If you're strong from the waist upwards, especially the shoulders, arms and neck muscles, you're able to concentrate better. This stands out at the beginning of each season. For the CanAm at Riverside at the end of October my neck never gets tired going round the loop at the end of the straight, but when we went there for Goodyear tyre testing in January, I found that my neck was getting really sore after the lay-off. It's the same at Indy. After a day's practice my head starts to ache with the strain; the next day it aches a little but not as much, and the next day it's better again. You must remember that a crash helmet, like the Bell Star I wear, weighs just over three pounds, and this is subjected to all the G-force loadings during braking, acceleration and cornering.

'The other thing I find tiring at the beginning of a season is trans-Atlantic jet travel, but here again you soon get used to it and it doesn't bother you. The more you do, the better you become adjusted. One thing I try and do on these long flights is to eat only when I ought to be eating – every four or five hours – and not every time they put a meal down in front of you. This way you can help to regulate yourself and not get caught on the time change which is the real problem. You gain five hours on the flight between London and New York, and across to Los Angeles it's nearly double that. Fortunately I can sleep on a plane.'

In 1968 Denny flew back and forth between Indianapolis and Monaco like a Boeing shuttlecock. He left Indianapolis on the Wednesday to qualify for the Monaco Grand Prix on Thursday

afternoon and Friday morning. He arrived back in Indianapolis on Friday night, qualified his Eagle on Saturday afternoon
and at 4.30pm he was in a helicopter heading for the airport
where a Lear jet was waiting to fly him to New York. A Boeing
707 to Milan was met at 8.15am Sunday morning by European
Cessna agent, Bob Williams, with a Cessna 411S for the hop to
Nice, and he was sitting down for breakfast with the slightly
incredulous McLaren crew at ten o'clock on the morning of the
race. He finished fifth in the Grand Prix after changing a broken
driveshaft during the race, and the next morning he was heading
back to Indianapolis again where he finished fourth in an Eagle.

'Trips like that do get to you,' admits Hulme. 'It's hard to
say how much but you're not as alert as you should be, because
all those time changes lumped together do affect you.'

There are two sides to Denis Hulme. One is the side the
racing fraternity sees – the ragged grin and the wave, the thin-
ning hair and the determination. But at home, Hulme mellows
to a slippered family man and father with his feet up watching
television, or worrying about progress on the modern new home
that is being built to his specifications at St George's Hill, in the
heart of Surrey's stockbroker belt. At airports, Denis is inclined
to buy or browse through magazines on houses and homemaking
rather than the horsepower press for the racing buffs. His father
talks of Denny's prowess in the family flower garden in New
Zealand, but at first glance Denis betrays no hint of a latent
green thumb. The apartment in Surbiton that he bought when
he and Greeta were married in 1963 had no flower garden, but
when Denis got to work one winter it had central heating. From
yards of copper piping Denis had plumbed the apartment with
a system that would have done credit to a qualified tradesman.

Denis is nobody's ideal as a swinging extrovert hellraising
racing driver. With few exceptions the modern successful driver
is a quiet-living professional. Denny drives a 3-litre Ford Zodiac
Executive and does not aspire to anything more sporty. Transport in comfort is what he requires. He gets his speed kicks
on the race tracks. He remembers Bruce, like Brabham, as a

slightly absent-minded driver on the road. 'He'd chat away going slowly for mile after mile and then suddenly he'd spear off in a burst of enthusiasm.'

I myself always had the impression driving with Bruce in his Mercedes that he felt he was driving down a one-way street and there would never be any cars coming the other way. His mind was invariably on other things. Denny agrees. 'That's right. He'd be chattering on about his theories on the latest projects that had caught his attention, and suddenly he'd jam on the brakes and say, "You drive. I'm going to sleep." And he'd climb over into the back seat and that'd be the last you'd hear from him.'

Accidents were generally things that happened to other people until the New Zealand Grand Prix in 1968 when his Formula 2 Brabham somersaulted after tangling with a slower car. Denis emerged battered and bruised with nothing broken except the car. The fire at Indianapolis put another crack in the cocoon of confidence that most drivers race in. If they did not have this confidence, they could never race. Denny says he does not take risks that can be avoided. He does not go out to practise in the rain unless it is absolutely necessary. He likes to make a personal check on the strength of the parts that go into the suspension of his car.

It almost comes down to the belief in their own white knight invincibility. 'It's strange. If you have a crash and walk away from it you're inclined to joke about it afterwards, and it doesn't really seem to sink in that you could have been killed. Bruce was testing the M8B CanAm car a year before his fatal crash at Goodwood, and he went off on the opposite side of the road. The tub was destroyed. A big rock went under the car and did a lot of damage. He was annoyed at the set-back to the test programme while the car was rebuilt, but he never thought anything about the fact that he'd hopped out of the wreck without getting hurt. And yet he could easily have gone off on the other side of the road where the marshal's post was, a year earlier. . . .'

9 Racing Mechanics and Tyler Alexander

Racing mechanics, whether they admit it or not, are a special breed of people. They have to be. The hours involved are as long as it takes to get the job done, and social life has to be put to one side. Dedication to the job in hand is everything. The glitter soon wears off all the foreign travel if the only touring you do is driving between the hotel and the track – and then that is usually after dark. It is a special job requiring special people to do it.

Bruce McLaren started his racing team off with his own personal mechanic, Wally Willmott, a New Zealander who came to England in 1962 having served a standard five-year apprenticeship as an auto electrician in Timaru and had raced his own Ford-engined special and a 500 Cooper-Norton. Wally was groomed as Bruce's personal mechanic and they established a considerable rapport which showed clearly in the impeccable standard of McLaren's small racing operation that visited the Tasman series with special Coopers. Bruce always maintained that the closest co-operation with key staff was important to a close-knit competitive racing team, and when Tyler Alexander joined the embryo McLaren Racing Team, following the death of 'his' driver Timmy Mayer, Bruce groomed the American and the New Zealander as an equal pair in his growing team.

The problem with forming close relationships in any form of business, as Bruce was to find out, is that the other part often does not place similar importance on the association. It may be important to the job in hand, but it does not always seem imperative to maintain the close liaison. To Bruce, it was always imperative if the job was to be done successfully. And this was why he took it as a personal blow when Wally Willmott left the team to get married and live in Australia in 1967, and when Robin Herd left to work with Cosworth.

The intercommunication of ideas between Tyler and Bruce was probably the most lasting liaison in the team and Tyler was elevated to chief mechanic, engineer in charge of the racing operations in all fields the team entered, and finally a director of the Company.

McLaren Racing is the only team which currently competes in Grand Prix, CanAm and Indianapolis-type racing but from a mechanic's viewpoint, Grand Prix training is the best background. 'We've got a better team in CanAm racing because a lot of the people that work on our CanAm cars used to work on the Formula 1 cars. The thing about Grand Prix racing that makes you a better mechanic is that it is so intensely competitive. You can't slow at all. You've got to try to be smarter. You've got to keep thinking about it. It's very hard work but it's so competitive that you develop a very competitive spirit and with this competitive spirit you develop a very competitive attitude. If you miss by a second because someone's forgotten something, you don't make the race, but in CanAm you can miss by ten seconds and still get in the race.

'It's difficult to explain,' says Alexander, 'if you're good you're good. If you're not very good or you're not as good as the other people in the team it shows up, and there are always a lot of people who are willing to work harder and take your place.

'Formula 1 cars are easier to work on than CanAm cars, but in Formula 1 you have to work much harder and faster. A CanAm sports car is more work taking it as a vehicle and we probably do more work between races on the CanAm cars than we do on Formula 1, but with Formula 1 the competition is so keen and so competitive that you've got to do things quickly and be sharp. Really on the ball. You can't mess around trying to make up your mind what to do when something goes wrong on the morning of a Grand Prix. You've got to say, "Do you think that's going to be better? Well, try it. Quick. Now! Because when you operate like that it could mean half a second somewhere in the race."

'If you're a good Formula 1 mechanic, you're pretty good at almost anything, but Indianapolis is a completely different deal. It's another kind of motor racing and patience is something you need there more than at any other race. The best thing about Formula 1 is that you can get on with it, but at Indy everything is such a long drawn-out process. Some of their rules are justified because Indy is a very dangerous place. You go very very fast in a confined area, much more so than on any Grand Prix or CanAm road circuit. The difficult thing for a mechanic is that in any other form of racing if you have a problem you drag out your toolbox and get after it, but at Indianapolis you have to pack everything up on the pit front and drag the car away to the garage area and do a fifteen-minute job in two hours. At a Formula 1 race there's no way you could take that long because you just wouldn't make the race . . .'

Like racing drivers, some of the better mechanics are probably born to it. They have the special blend of tolerance and talents that are required to keep them on the job and on the rails working under tension and strain for much of the time. But good racing mechanics can also be made with proper training. Care, thoroughness and dedication are the main requirements. Tyler Alexander studied aircraft engineering when he left school and this instilled thoroughness as well as teaching him the technical skills of welding, fabricating sheet metal, and the practical side of engineering as applied to building airplanes. Inadvertently it was the ideal background for a modern racing mechanic in an era when design in racing is linking closer with airplane principles.

'If someone was to ask me what was the best training for a racing mechanic I'd tell them to go to an aircraft engineering school. You learn to be a lot more careful, and more precise because when one of those things quits in the air you don't just get out and fix it. So you have to make sure that it doesn't quit.

After a while you develop the attitude that it's not so much knowing what's wrong when it goes wrong (although it does help!) as doing it right in the first place so that it doesn't go wrong.'

This sort of training is probably better for a racing mechanic than perhaps the more usual garage apprenticeship, as Tyler points out. 'Alastair Caldwell, our chief Formula 1 mechanic, possibly knows more about cars as cars than I do because he was an apprentice in a big garage in New Zealand and when a Jaguar comes in making a weird noise he knows that it's got a busted framstat. I wouldn't have a goddam clue what was wrong with it because I've never had anything to do with standard road cars. It's either been a racing car, or I'd just as soon not bother . . .'

Alexander's career as a racing engineer grew without a great deal of apparent patterned planning. After he completed his pressure-cooker two-year course at the aircraft engineering school he 'just sort of bummed around'. He was not particularly interested in a nine-to-five job and the excitement of motor racing offered more interest to a twenty-one-year old. The guys he hung around with in his hometown (Hingham, Mass.) were all interested in flying and they were also racing specials that they had built themselves. One of the part-time race driver/flyers, John Fields, decided to get more serious at the racing game and bought a 500cc Cooper-Norton and with Tyler looking after the little Formula 3 car during the 1961 season they ran seventeen races with fifteen wins in the national championship. The Mayer brothers, Timmy and Teddy, were running a Formula Junior Cooper with Timmy driving and Teddy looking after the team management and quite often Fields and Mayer were running in the same race, but in different classes. He did not have anything to do at the end of the season, so Tyler took the Mayers' Cooper down to Nassau where Roger Penske drove it because Timmy was serving his stint in the army. 'I wasn't really working for Teddy as a mechanic, but I just sort of ended up taking the car to several races and started working for Teddy without ever having said, "How about a job?" or anything like that. It just happened.'

Tyler worked for John Mecom's team when Roger Penske was driving the Zerex Special – a car that was to be the forerunner of all the McLaren sports cars. In fact Tyler had helped to rebuild the Cooper as a single-seater Formula 1 car after Walter Hansgen had wrecked it in the U.S. Grand Prix at Watkins Glen, and Timmy Mayer had driven the car on occasions. Later the single-seater was converted to a centre-seater sports car and driven with great flair by Penske, winning most of the big-money sports car races before regulations forced him to alter the car to a more legal two-seater. It made the Zerex Special no less competitive and Tyler was working on the crew when Penske won the Guards Trophy race at Brands Hatch in 1963. Having fulfilled his commitment to Uncle Sam, Timmy Mayer had been driving a Formula Junior Cooper for Ken Tyrrell during 1963 and with his wife Garrell and brother Teddy they were living in a rented house on an island in the River Thames. Tyler renewed his association with the Mayers and decided to join up with them again, so he resigned from Mecom's team and accompanied the Mayers to a race in Copenhagen instead of returning to America.

Bruce McLaren came round to one of the riverside lunch parties hobbling on a cane after a frightening end-over-end crash in the German Grand Prix to continue discussions about taking a pair of 2.5 litre Cooper-Climaxes to New Zealand and Australia for the Tasman series during January and February in 1965. Wally Willmott was building Bruce's car – a special slimline lightweight with minimum tankage – at the Cooper Car Company in Surbiton, and Tyler joined him to start building a twin car for Timmy.

'To me, Coopers were a big deal in those days because we had been running the 500, the Formula Junior and the Formula 1 car in the States, but it didn't seem to be such a big deal when I actually went into the shop.'

The staff at the Cooper Car Company in those days was

something of an institution, having been with the firm since
Charles Cooper first capitalized on his idea to use Fiat 500 front
suspension units front and rear on a lightweight frame and fit it
with a motorcycle engine to build a cheap, sturdy, competitive
car for Formula 3 racing. When Tyler arrived, the racing
factory had not changed a lot since those early days. The old
hands were probably openly critical about American racing
people who often arrived with more money than driving ability
and certainly only a modicum of mechanical skills. Tyler was
an exception. 'I was amazed at the time, that there was a
bunch of people working away in a dirty dark corner of the
world and I had been tossed in there by Timmy and Teddy to
get on with the job and these people were very impressed that I
could actually weld and do something!

'Bruce was in and out of the factory all the time and the cars
were being built, but I don't ever remember being formally
introduced, and at the time I didn't know a great deal about
him. In fact I was fairly ignorant about the whole business but
I was keen on doing something I was interested in and these
people seemed to be very serious about what they were doing,
so I thought it would be a good bunch to kind of tag along
behind. There were so many things that I didn't know about
racing cars then and this guy with the limp seemed to know a
fair bit about them so I thought maybe I'd better pay a bit of
attention to him and see what was going on.'

From these early days working on the Tasman Coopers,
Tyler stayed with Bruce as he built up the team, working first in
New Malden, then in Feltham, and finally at the more exten-
sive, expensive factory where the team is currently based at
Colnbrook.

'Bruce was very easy to learn from, but I find now that I
didn't really learn all that much and I think I know why. After
working for him for about a year and a half I found that I was
doing my part of the job and he was doing his. I knew that the
car had to be finished and had to be at the race and I knew how
he wanted it, but we were kind of working in parallel rather

'than together. Well, maybe parallel isn't quite right. Maybe it was together. We used to argue like hell over how something should be done, but we never seemed to get upset about it, and we always ended up with a reasonable solution. He knew what he wanted and after a couple of years I believed him. It's odd thinking back, because we used to argue like hell but we never said, well screw you because I'm going to do it my way, and I guess that's why we got on so well together.

'I realize now that I should have learned more from Bruce. I got on with my own job, and never reckoning he was going to write himself off, I never bothered to get him to explain a lot of the technical or engineering to me because he knew that part. That was his department. I could cope with the detail bits and pieces and making sure that the car was built, and he did the other part of saying *we* should put that there, or *why* don't we mount that there? And I would say well Gee we did that last year and it's no good and remembered why it was no good. . . .

'This is why I felt out of place after Bruce's death. He and I had worked so much as a team that I hadn't bothered to pay much attention to the things he did as long as the end result was right. Now I have to work with the designers and try to communicate the things that I learnt on the practical side and hope that they can cope with the other side of it. I've also got to communicate what the drivers comment on the feel of the car, back to the designers. It's worked out that I've fallen into doing this without even trying. All of a sudden this is what I'm doing . . . I'm director of the company and I never set out to do that . . . I was interested in doing a job . . . I wanted to win. I reckon if you've got enough initiative to want to get on, there's no reason why you shouldn't finish up owning the place.'

Tyler's career in McLaren Racing may not be the logical climax of career for every mechanic who gets involved in motor racing but a basic technical grounding and initiative obviously help. Jim Hall's German Chaparral mechanics, Tyler points out, are among the best in the racing game and they learnt a lot by being trained Volkswagen mechanics.

'Their Volkswagen training taught them to be thorough and not to forget things. If you were to say that racing mechanics should have any special talent, it is basically to be very very thorough and not to forget things because you don't get another chance to fix them once the race starts.'

Aircraft engineering and Volkswagen training are two avenues suggested as good backgrounds to being a racing mechanic, but Tyler also points to Team Lotus. 'Lotus have very good racing mechanics. It seems to me that when they first go there they don't have anything over anyone else but they *know* that Colin Chapman is very good – they may not like him, but they know he's good – and quite a few of the Lotus mechanics have ended up being very, very good. They respect Colin Chapman because he's had years and years of experience. They believe in him and they learn from him. Maybe part of this is that Lotus have always had very good drivers and when you're working with someone who is capable of winning a race and is giving it their 100 per cent, then you give him your 100 per cent. If you're working for a driver who isn't going to make it, it's easy to say, ah, why the hell bother working all night for him – he's not going to win the race anyway . . . Chapman has always managed to have that air of success about him or at least had good people driving for him, and . . . y'know . . . I think good people go together.

'I always felt that when I was working with Timmy and later with Bruce. I didn't know anything and Timmy didn't know anything, but we said we'd have a stab at getting to the top together. I suppose it ended up happening with Bruce because later we used to laugh and say well, we're on our way. Let's not stop now. We'll bust our ass till we beat them all. . . .'

Tyler lived with Bruce and Patty McLaren when they moved from Surbiton to Walton-on-Thames, and Tyler and Bruce absorbed each other's racing lore and invented new philosophy after late dinners when they had arrived back from the workshop. 'We used to say if there was a race tomorrow with a bunch of nobodies in the field and they paid twenty thousand dollars to win, or there was a race tomorrow with Jack Brabham, Jochen Rindt, Jimmy Clark and Jackie Stewart running, which race would you go to? We would reckon that we'd be at the race where the Brabhams and the Stewarts and the rest of them were at, because they were the guys to beat. You want to win, but you want to win against the best people. We used to joke about it, but we still agreed on it. I want to win, but I want to beat someone doing it. I don't just want to simply win. It's a bit like in *The Money Game* – winning is just a means of keeping score, and the better guys you beat, the better score you get.'

Getting to the stage where you share in a successful driver's career and business and thoughts is one side of the penny, but it is a hard slog. A racing mechanic works endless hours – a lot of round-the-clock 'all-nighters' – to get his car to the line, and he bears a lot of responsibility. The elation conquers the weariness as the race starts, but it changes to concern that all will go well with their car and they have to live with the nagging worry that something might happen. Something that could be the fault of something he forgot to do. Tyler Alexander says this is a worry that a racing mechanic always has to live with. A mental cross he has to bear.

'It scares the hell out of me all the time when I think of what could happen during a race. I worry about what could fall off the thing, y'know, it's a lethal weapon. It's a fairly dangerous piece of equipment. I guess nobody ever says anything about it, because nobody ever says anything about people getting killed in motor racing. They say, well it'll never happen to *me*. I don't know whether it's like this with other mechanics but if the car has a shunt or something the first thing that always flashes through my mind is, Christ, what did I forget that time. I must say, as far as I know anyway, I've never forgotten anything that has caused something to happen, but it's always the first thing that flashes through our mind because there are so many things. You notice during a race that perhaps some of the mechanics give the impression that they don't give a damn, but you know that they do.'

If the mechanics on a racing team worry during a race it stands to reason that a driver know of this worry and he worries too. The topline drivers drive for topline teams and they can luxuriate in the knowledge that their car has been prepared by the top mechanics, but there are drivers who, because of intimate mechanical knowledge or a nervous need to assure themselves, double-check their cars before a race. This is nerve-wrecking for mechanics because it shows a basic distrust of their ability, even though it is probably no more than a habit that the driver has formed over the years with various teams. For the driver it is a part of the ritual of preparing for a race; for the mechanics it is a niggling phobia.

'I guess some of the drivers worry about their cars – the ones that know what's going on, anyways. Bruce was obviously one of the drivers who knew what was going on and what it took to prepare a car and that there were mechanical things and that somebody's hands actually did do up nuts and bolts and things. But some drivers just front up and sit in the car and ask you which way the track goes. Maybe that doesn't happen so much nowadays when it has gotten so competitive, and it is essential that a driver knows more about what goes on.

'I've never worked with a driver like this, but there are drivers who ask various questions before they get in the car – did you remember to do this, and did you remember to do that? It's something in the back of their head that they worry about – it's a psychological thing, I suppose, where they have a pet worry. They ask the same questions every single time they get in the car.

'Bruce was never that way. He might ask similar sorts of questions, but it was never the same thing every time. He would ask perhaps about a specific problem from the night before. "Were you able to fix such-and-such, and if you weren't, were you able to fix it well enough so that it'll finish the race?" That sort of thing. . . .'

Between races the McLaren team mechanics check everything that is feasible to check on the cars, but their programme rather depends on the amount of time they have available. If time permits, the parts that have been dismantled are sent out to be magnafluxed, or visually checked for any sign of a failure or the possible start of a tiny crack or a flaw in the material.

'In aircraft terminology we call this preventive maintenance. Even if there's nothing wrong, you pull it apart and make sure there's nothing wrong or likely to go wrong. We try to do more and better preventive maintenance than other teams.'

The suspension is completely rebuilt between races. The suspension comes off the car and the uprights come completely apart. All the steel parts are magnafluxed and all the magnesium or non-ferrous metal parts are Zyglowed. Generally the mechanics know which are the problem areas and these are the areas that are checked first. If there has been a transmission problem then the gearbox comes off first and is completely taken apart and checked.

'You develop priorities working on a car from experience and problems in the past, and you work from that. You have a standard list of things you try and do between races. We have a standard procedure with a check-list that we try to stay reasonably close to, say, the night before a race. If there are no problems in the car, it's a list that takes roughly four or five hours to check through. It includes taking a thorough look at the gearbox, a good look round the motor, a general check of all the brake system, the chassis itself for any physical damage, checking anything that might have happened in practice, checking the fuel system and calculating the fuel mileage from fuel checks in practice, and charging the battery for the car. These are things that most teams do as a matter of course.'

Long working hours tend to cancel the more glamorous attractions of being a racing mechanic as far as the average garage mechanic is concerned, but rebuilding a car between practice and the race, that could involve working all night, or all night all the next day and the next night as well to get the car on the line, is taken as part of the job. How do such hours affect a mechanic? Does it have an adverse effect on the job he does?

'It bothers you, yeah, when your hands get fuzzy and your teeth feel furry and your eyes get a bit blurred, but I guess although you complain about it like hell, way in the back of your mind, as long as you've got a chance of winning the race you just keep doing it because you know it's got to be done. If you can do a job within reasonable sort of working hours, fine, but if it takes three days and three nights nonstop to have it done by Friday morning at ten o'clock because that's when it has to be done, then whatever it takes to be done by then, that's what it takes. . . .

'The only reason you ever stop working on a racing car is because the guy drops the starting flag. Long hours affect different people different ways. It often depends on whether you're winning or losing. It's great after two or three all-nighters if you win the race or if you think you have a chance of winning the race. You may be completely buggered and collapse, but you collapse with a smile on your face!'

A close-knit relationship, a sense of trust, between the racing driver and the mechanics working on his car is important. Any bickering or a lack of confidence from either side and it gives the driver a new worry which can sometimes take the edge off his performance. One of the reasons for success with the McLaren team is the 'family' relationship. Everyone knew everyone else was giving the project their utmost and at races you could almost feel a sense of high spirits. The drivers entered into this and were responsible for keeping spirits bouyant. Mechanics often have a keener sense of being able to rate a driver than perhaps outside observers do, and Tyler was of the opinion that although Denny Hulme was usually quicker than Bruce in the Formula 1 cars, Bruce was more often faster in CanAm racing and he was easier on the cars. 'Bruce was always very easy on the equipment, but perhaps that's not very fair as a comparison because Denny isn't hard on the equipment or the car. Bruce was easier to work with because ninety per cent of the time he knew what was going on with the car and he knew how he wanted it fixed. That's not putting Denny down in any way, because as a race driver he could charge harder than Bruce usually – it was just that he didn't have Bruce's engineering background.

'If Bruce had set the car up the way he wanted it, Denny could climb in and drive it for a few laps and he would like it as well. Most times Denny was content to drive the car the way Bruce set it up, and quite often he was quicker than Bruce.

'Bruce was very consistent, but he obviously enjoyed driving the big powerful CanAm cars more than he did the Formula 1 cars where you had to be more precise. He enjoyed something you could pitch and toss around, something that you could drive more with your right foot than with precise movements of the steering wheel.' Tyler's view from the pits contradicts Denny's cockpit opinion.

In the early stages of the team, with the notable exception of Tyler and, for a time, of Gary Knutson who came from Chaparral and later rejoined the Texan team, Bruce favoured hiring New Zealand mechanics. This was not just a national bias, it was a hunch Bruce had that mechanics who learned their trade in New Zealand probably were more able to think for themselves, to innovate, and to improvise, than were their English equivalents. In New Zealand replacement parts were not always readily available so the broken part either had to be rebuilt or a new part made from scratch. When Bruce needed a new cylinder head for his little Ulster Austin a replacement part was out of the question so he set about welding and filing until he had completely rebuilt the old head to his own design. This was the sort of initiative he expected the mechanics on his racing team to have and he reasoned that New Zealanders were more likely to share his sort of background experience.

As the McLaren team outgrew the New Malden tractor shed and moved to the 4,000 sq. ft. factory in Feltham, the staff grew to include Bruce Harre (now a technician with Firestone), Howden Ganley who is now a racing driver in his own right with sponsored drives in Formula 1 and Formula 5,000, and Colin Beanland who had accompanied Bruce to England in 1958. It was generally understood that Colin Beanland had received a fee from the 'Driver to Europe' scholarship to work as Bruce's racing mechanic on the Formula 2 1,500cc Cooper-Climax he drove that year, but of course Beanland paid his own fare and assisted Bruce where he could on the preparation of the car since he had had no training as a mechanic. Bruce, then, at twenty-one started his racing career in Europe as a driver who also looked after his own car.

As McLaren Racing went from success to success the staff grew and Harry Pearce, an ex-motorcycle racer, and a racing mechanic who had looked after Bruce's Cooper when he drove for English entrant, Tommy Atkins, joined as workshop manager. At the time of Bruce's death, the staff numbered fifty-five including eight on the CanAm sports car crew in America and six at the engine shop in Detroit where Colin Beanland is now workshop manager.

Tyler Alexander has not changed much since he first joined the McLaren team as a twenty-four-year-old in 1964. He still has a passion for cleanliness on the workshop floor and either works on the cars in a white shop coat, or in jeans and a jersey and a scuffed pair of handmade Italian Gucci shoes. The Rolex watch does not really match the manual work, but it fits the picture better when he switches roles, climbing the stairs to his desk and discussing policy with the other directors or sitting down to a think session with the designers.

Tyler Alexander is a racing mechanic who has made good.

10 *Internal Business Management with Phil Kerr*

'When Bruce first mentioned to me that he was leaving Coopers and going on his own, I had my doubts and told him so . . .' Phil Kerr, then business manager for Jack Brabham was well aware of the problems involved in getting started with a new team. He had been closely involved when Jack left the Cooper team to set up his own racing organization in 1962.

'I didn't feel that Bruce was ready for it at that stage because I thought he was too young. On reflection this was unfair judgment because when Jack went on his own he was a good deal older than Bruce – he was thirty-two – and for this reason I thought Bruce in his mid-twenties was trying to do too much.'

Phil was studying accountancy when he first met Bruce at the Muriwai hillclimb. When he was eighteen he left college to join the New Zealand Forest Service as a clerk, going to university after work. At this stage he was also secretary of the Auckland Car Club, the largest car club in the country, and on the board of control of the International Grand Prix Association. Phil left the Forest Service to join Arthur Harris, who had a small engineering business and handled Buckler sales in New Zealand.

'It was beginning to get to the stage where cars and engineering were of more interest to me than pure accounting. I've never really enjoyed pure accounting because I've never had the patience to sit at a desk all day long and balance books. That's why I've always inclined towards business management studies rather than pure economics, because management offers a lot more in terms of allowing you to express ideas, and allowing you to do things other than pure accounting. But you need accounting as a basic background. It teaches you the basic principles and rules.'

Bruce had mentioned to Jack that Phil was interested in some form of management job in England and since Jack was branching out into other activities and business ventures he asked Phil to come over in 1959.

As a business organizer then, Bruce was an extremely good racing driver, and his talents developed more towards engineering and design than towards the business side of racing. 'He didn't really need to be a businessman in those days because he was getting paid as a driver and his income was all fairly straightforward. In later years he found that he had to become a little more interested in business activities, but I don't believe that business was ever his strong forte. He was able to analyse business situations on information he had in front of him, but he never had the patience in that area as he had in others to seek out the information that was required relative to the needs of the business. But if a lot of the basic work was done he was able to assess it, and he was able to make very sensible decisions. When I joined his company, Bruce became chairman and I was joint managing director with Teddy Mayer. What I tried to do with Bruce was to feed him information about what was happening in all the areas under my jurisdiction and then let him make decisions based on that information.'

The news that Bruce was thinking of leaving the Cooper team to concentrate on building his own cars came as something of a surprise to the man in whose footsteps Bruce had been following for several years.

'Jack was a little surprised,' Phil recalls, 'but he had known Bruce long enough to be aware of his abilities. However, I don't think Jack envisaged that Bruce was going to be as dominant in some areas of racing and to produce such good motor cars in such a relatively short space of time. I don't think anybody thought Bruce would be capable of producing cars of the calibre and quality that he subsequently did.'

It was Phil who had been largely responsible for Denny

Hulme getting his chance in the Brabham team, and in addition to his position with Jack and his companies, Phil was also looking after Denny's interests. When Denny left the Brabham team to join Bruce at the end of 1967, Phil was in a delicate position of divided loyalty and he was soon to follow Denny into the McLaren fold.

The arrangement, although appearing cumbersome at first, in fact settled down quickly with Teddy Mayer concentrating on the increased activities of the team in North America, and Phil Kerr looking after the administration of the factory on a day-to-day basis and also the Formula 1 programme. They were each experts in their own fields and the division worked out well.

'The general administration of the company is pretty much the same as any other commercial organization. The fact that it's a racing team presents certain complications, but generally normal business methods apply. It's important to keep the company organized using good basic commercial principles. We've endeavoured to improve the efficiency of the company as a whole. We've known that internal communication between the various personnel is important and while this had tended to be overlooked, it is now vastly improved. It was also necessary to improve the efficiency of the financial control.'

Like Topsy, the McLaren team has just growed, with the design, building, development, and racing of cars as the prime aim to the exclusion of almost anything else. Not until the company staff had reached double figures was the suggestion of a holiday met with anything more than an incredulous glance from Bruce. Vacations were regarded with the same scorn as the suggestion of an eight-hour day. When the tiny team had started the hours involved were as long as it took to get a job done and all-nighters were taken for granted. With three or four on the staff the involvement with Bruce on a personal level was compensation enough, but as the team grew and the personal relationship was diluted a little, more 'civilized' habits started to creep into the operation.

'Motor racing is a bit odd in that quite apart from trying to operate as a normal company, there is always an unknown element in it. You can never be sure of the really immediate future of racing, and it is becoming more expensive every year. In addition to finding the necessary finance to operate the team each year, it becomes increasingly important to control that finance.'

Formula 1 racing has its own particular problems. The season lasts from March through October and in that time a group of men and equipment has to be moved from South Africa, around most of Europe, and eventually across to Canada, the United States and Mexico. The rest of the year is used up with design, building and development of new cars for the coming season and for the workshop staff this can be as hectic as it is for the race crews when the 'circus' gets on the move during the season.

Planning for the coming season is usually started six months beforehand when the international calendar is published and arrangements are made for hotel accommodation and for garage facilities.

This is a field where experience is important. 'In addition to hotels and garages you also have to plan a movements schedule which covers flights for drivers and others who may be flying to the races; you have to arrange the channel crossings for the transporter and the accompanying vehicles, and also the customs documents and insurance papers that may be required at each border.' Phil is known as 'Sunny Tours' when the race crews are on the move. . . .

When the scene switches to North America, all the competing Formula 1 cars are carried on a charter flight to Canada, and are then trucked together down to Watkins Glen in New York State and finally hauled down to Mexico. The Formula 1 Constructors' Association gets together on documentation for this section of the season, but it is still an enormous job as the McLaren Team ships thirty crates of spares in addition to the cars and spare engines, and the mechanics have to be familiar with the placing of all the important components. This is where the chief mechanics of racing teams have to become tour managers as well as being responsible for the preparation of the cars. When the transporter leaves the factory, the chief mechanic – Alastair Caldwell in the McLaren Formula 1 team – is responsible for the smooth-running of the trip. All possible documentation is provided for him, and he then has to see that the entourage reaches the race track.

'Alastair and the other mechanics cope well with the paper-work at the borders now, purely as a result of experience in this area, and they have come to know the best approach to the various customs offices,' says Phil.

Experience is certainly the best teacher. 'None of the problems are particularly difficult – the problems that arise now can easily be overcome by application. When I first started working for Jack Brabham the understanding of all the different customs requirements for the various countries was a serious obstacle to overcome, but with experience these have become straightforward. It's easy enough to phone the relevant embassy or check with the Royal Automobile Club if you are in doubt on any point.

'Quite often for Spain or France or Italy you have to apply for documentation anything up to three months ahead. If you leave it till the last minute, the chances are you won't get what's required and your transporter and mechanics won't get through to the race. You have the responsibility of ensuring that when the transporter leaves the factory (and usually the crew is very tired perhaps after an all-nighter on final preparations) that everything goes as smoothly as possible.'

Any forward-thinking racing organization must consider the prospects of diversification in the future with a view to exploring other avenues connected with motor racing, and for the McLaren team the most obvious dream was a McLaren road car just as Colin Chapman's Lotus racing team had grown to build the Elites, Elans, Sevens and Europas in addition to their racing activities.

'We had felt for some time that we shouldn't just rely on

racing entirely for the future, and that we should have other commercial activities, either in the nucleus stage or at least with a possibility of being developed over the next few years, so that we could become self-sufficient as an organization without depending entirely on going racing. Whilst we were interested in going racing, it would have to be number one priority because (a) it is an image builder and (b) it provides the bulk of the income which would ultimately be applied to other projects. In any case winning and being competitive and expanding the name was very important to Bruce and to the team. I know Bruce got nearly as much enjoyment from seeing the cars do well and seeing a McLaren car win races as he probably did from winning a race himself with his own car. It was a symbol of success. The fact that the name McLaren was becoming increasingly well known, particularly in North America, was due to the success of the cars as much as to Bruce's own success as a driver in CanAm, and this was important to him.'

The company is still working on long-term projects but the dream of the road car has been shelved, for the moment.

In five years the McLaren organization mushroomed from the tractor shed in New Malden, through the narrow factory in Feltham, to the relative luxury of a 7,000 sq. ft. factory at Colnbrook, near the little old village that grew up from a coaching stop on the road from London to Bath. The runways of London's Heathrow airport are deafeningly close. Immediate plans are for a move to an even larger 11,000 sq. ft. factory which the company has purchased freehold, rather than pay the high rents for industrial property in the area. The new factory is only one hundred yards along David Road from the existing premises, has three drawing offices and three management offices upstairs, with a further four offices downstairs. Out in the workshops there will be a greater area in which the three separate teams as well as the prototype build programme can operate.

At the end of the 1970 season the team staff numbered 42. Teddy Mayer, Phil Kerr and Tyler Alexander are the three directors and they are assisted by an accountant and by Sue Winslade who acts as secretary to all three. There are three designers and two draughtsmen in the drawing offices. Downstairs is the office of general manager Harry Pearce, who looks after purchasing and engineering procurement. He has an assistant who is also in charge of quality control, checking on everything that is made in the workshops and everything that is bought-out.

Don Beresford, who worked as a racing mechanic with Aston Martin and Lola before joining the McLaren team, is works foreman and has general authority over all the workshop in addition to his special department looking after the building of the prototype McLarens behind the high wall at the end of the factory. There are three machinists, two sheet metal workers, two welders, and two general personnel in the build shop as well as a specialist fitter. Each racing team has about five mechanics, and there are 'floating' personnel who are available to help whichever department needs assistance. To keep the team transport rolling there is a vehicles manager who looks after servicing and the loading of the transporter as well as the other vehicles. He also looks after the stores.

The giant Ford Transporter holds three cars and most of the spares required for a Grand Prix, but it requires careful loading with spare engines, transmissions, suspension parts, spare body sections, wheels and the million other parts to keep a racing team mobile away from the base.

The McLaren fleet consists of the transporter, an Econoline van that often accompanies the 'mother ship' to the races along with a Ford Transit, two Ford Thames vans, four Mini vans, and four staff cars. Nearing the start of the racing season there can be anything up to ten new racing cars in the workshop as the crews prepare for Formula 1, CanAm and Indianapolis.

Since the McLaren team is the only racing organization to compete in these three major fields in North America and in Europe, there have been suggestions that the Grand Prix team could be dropped in favour of the more lucrative forms of racing in the United States, but Teddy Mayer discounts this on purely economic grounds.

'Surprisingly enough the possible income from racing in Formula 1 and racing in CanAm is fairly equal, when you take the guaranteed start monies as well as the prize and bonus monies you earn in Formula 1 as opposed to the prize money only from the CanAm races. However, I would say that probably two-thirds of our sponsorship is in fact allocated to us by our sponsors because we are going racing in CanAm rather than in Formula 1.

'If we were to cut out Formula 1 we would find that the number of designers, the size of the plant, the number of build personnel, the number of mechanics – our basic overheads – would not be a great deal smaller. And the addition of the income which Formula 1 provides would more than cover that difference. Let's say all three of our racing projects cost equal amounts. In fact they do. They cost within about ten per cent of each other. If you stop doing one, your income would be cut by a third, but your costs would only be cut by about fifteen per cent. Your rent and rates and this sort of thing would be virtually the same. There would be some small savings – you wouldn't need the same number of mechanics, for instance – but costing it out carefully you'd save only about a sixth and you'd lose about a third of your income.'

When the McLaren team first started to become successful in CanAm racing, Bruce put a lot of the credit down to their participation in Grand Prix racing with its spur to mechanical and design development, but by the start of the 1970 season he felt the rub-off between Grand Prix and CanAm was starting to even itself up. The M15 Indianapolis car probably owed more to the CanAm sports car than it did to the M7 Formula 1 car.

'I think we're probably learning as much from the CanAm cars,' said Bruce. 'Although it hasn't been competitive racing we've always run fairly hard in practice and we've always tried as hard as we can in terms of experiments and developments on the cars. We never set ourselves limits on design time or money that we've been prepared to spend on the CanAm car. I think the M8 sports car is a much better car in terms of design than the old M7 Formula 1, because that was basically a copy of our Formula 2 car and that was never very good.'

In terms of time Bruce McLaren achieved a tremendous amount in a short period. He left the Cooper Formula 1 team at the end of 1965 to devote all his attention to his own racing team, and when he did so he surprised more people than Jack Brabham and Phil Kerr. It seems hard to believe that in four summers he developed his own new cars and a brand new reputation for himself as an engineer and car-builder as well as a racing driver and patron of a team.

'Bruce's future was unlimited,' says Phil. 'Apart from the fact that we will miss him, I think the saddest thing is that while we appreciate the years that he was around, we can only wonder about the years during which I think he would have done so much more. I believe that his talents were yet to show to the full. He was just beginning to show the signs of being an innovator. He felt that he had served another apprenticeship – a sort of extension of his earlier driver's apprenticeship – as a constructor, and he had jumped the first hurdle which involved engineering and designing good sound safe motorcars.

'He was learning all the time. He had this marvellous attribute of being able to retain information, assimilating all manner of engineering knowledge. He would watch what other people were doing and analyse it, rejecting what he didn't like and retaining what he did, storing it for future use.

'His imagination was working all the time. It didn't matter if you were with Bruce on an aeroplane, at his home, or out to dinner, he would always be mulling over particular problems or cars or future projects that he might have been reminded of during the course of conversation.

'Ranked with the other leading designers of our time Bruce had some remarkable achievements to his credit at thirty-two. At that age both Brabham and Colin Chapman were only just beginning. They had a long start on Bruce and it wasn't until their late thirties or early forties that they came to be really widely recognized for their talents. Bruce had done so much by this time that it is really difficult to know how much he might have achieved by the time he reached his early forties. We can only surmise. I think that Bruce would probably have surpassed the efforts of all his contemporaries and that the McLaren organization would have been a team to be even more proud of.'

11 Racing from Behind the Pit Wall

The McLaren domination in the CanAm sports car series has been likened to the Mercedes-Benz supremacy in Grand Prix racing in the late thirties and the mid-fifties. The Mercedes reputation grew from the strict and efficient team management of Neubauer and the same clinical attention to detail is a factor in the dominance of Team McLaren in the North American sports car races.

In private testing sessions and during race practice, every modification or change to the car is noted on a Vehicle Running Record along with drivers' comments and individual lap times. These records are filed for reference and in this way complete details of a car's behaviour under certain conditions can be checked at a later date.

This Vehicle Running Record was laid out and produced by Teddy Mayer. Spaces are provided for the date, circuit, event, car, driver, weather, circuit length, total laps, total miles, fastest lap, average lap, water temperature, oil temperature, oil pressure and fuel pressure. And that is merely the heading line! Below that comes the tyre section with spaces for progressive records on temperature, pressure, camber and wear. Then there are lines numbered one through fifty with a space for the lap time and room to write in alterations and the effects and driver comments.

The back of the sheet is made up of the Vehicle Specification Record which is filled out after the race with intimate details of the setting-up of the racing car. Spaces record the date, track, event, car, driver, recorder, weather and temperature, then chassis number, engine number and gearbox number. The overall ratio comes next, then crownwheel and pinion ratio, and the individual ratios of each of the four or five gears.

There is a section for ignition timing, spark plugs, and fuel system, then details of wheels and tyres and notes on castor, toe-in, springs, roll-bars, ride height and wheel-weights with notes on different settings front and rear or from side to side. The condition of brake cylinder, clutch cylinder, front and rear brakes head the second column, followed by the settings for camber, shocks, and spring length front and rear. Spaces are left to note additional specifications, difficulties that might have been encountered with equipment, and any further general comments.

'The reason we keep such detailed charts of all the testing and practice is because the whole subject of setting up a race car and getting the last little bit of performance from it, is extremely complex,' says Mayer. 'The set-up on the car is completely inter-related. The front toe-in is related to the front camber which may be related to the castor which is related to the particular tyre you have on the car whose performance is related not only to the width of the front rim, but also to the width of the rear rim which in turn is related to the pressure of the tyres front and rear and to the geometry of the car. . . . This complexity means that each change has to be carefully noted so that you are able to get back to a particular condition where you felt the car was working particularly well on a particular track.'

These charts are not kept as reference for a track from year to year apart from basic information like gear ratios. The main purpose is a detailed record for use at the next race. 'The reason for this is that in twelve months you will have changed tyre sizes and tyre construction and other things about the car so much that you really only have a small amount of information which will be useful at the track by next season. In other words we couldn't come back to, say, Spa, and use an eighth toe-in because that's what we used last year. What we could do is reason that last year we started with no toe-in and found that an eighth toe-in worked, so this year maybe more toe-in at the front will help whatever condition develops at Spa. In other words,' reasons Mayer, 'you use the changes that you make at the track to guide you towards changes to make again at that track, rather than absolute identical settings.' '

Since these recording sheets were first used by the McLaren team they have been expanded to contain more and more different kinds of information with greater attention now being paid to tyre details and to aerodynamics behaviour on the car.

With a brand new McLaren on a test day the car is run for a few quiet warm-up laps to make sure there are no oil or water leaks, to bed the brakes, and to let the driver get comfortable. Perhaps the windscreen height has to be altered, some extra padding needed in the seat, or slight adjustments made to the position of the pedals. The driver then gradually builds up his speed with the car until he is going as fast as he can with the car set-up in that particular configuration. Then the test session really starts from this baseline condition. An alteration is made, and if only a small improvement is made or the driver is not absolutely sure that the change was for the better, the car is returned to its baseline condition again for a back-to-back comparison. If a change is made and it results in an enormous improvement this then becomes the baseline condition. In this context an enormous improvement could be half a second over a ten-lap period, while a small improvement would be an average of a tenth or a fifth of a second over the same distance.

This means that the results of a test session depend to a great extent on the ability of the driver. He does not have to be an engineering boffin to assist in the programme, but this obviously helps and in the case of Bruce McLaren it was invaluable assistance.

The basic requirement of a test driver is the ability to repeat his times for lap after lap, so that an improvement made on the car should show up as a consistent improvement on the test sheet. A fast driver is not necessarily a good driver for this sort of testing work, consistency is more important than out and out pace, which might not always reflect the changes that are being made.

Where Bruce was concerned he knew what was being done to the car and why, and he could analyse what difference this was making to the handling of the car while he was out on the circuit. Denny Hulme, on the other hand, is able to reel off a series of laps at a consistent speed and the worth of any alterations to the car are always reflected in his lap times.

Tyler Alexander is fond of describing the way good preparation helps enormously in a successful racing team by saying that you can screw up a car beyond belief given twenty seconds with a seven-sixteenth wrench. It's as easy to make alterations the wrong way and ruin the setting-up if you do not approach test sessions with great care. It is also easy to be misled by behaviour of the car or of the driver.

'At Indianapolis we found that just one turn on a spring abutment could mean two or three miles an hour – and that's a tremendous amount at Indy. If you change the rate of springs or make just a tiny adjustment you can get the thing completely out of the ball park,' says Mayer.

'We're dependent on what the driver says and how he feels. We can set the car up to the last tiny fraction of a degree in every direction, and each measurement can be exactly right, but if the driver's information as to whether the car feels secure, feels stable, is handling well or not, is wrong for any given reason, you can find that you're just going round in circles and no engineer in the world can tell you how to fix it.

'Indy is a perfect example of this. You can go out with a car that is set up to run at 168mph and the driver has no problem lapping at that speed. But the next day because the driver is slightly tired or not trying quite so hard – just a very slight difference – the car will only run 165 and the driver will say it feels terrible when in fact you haven't changed a thing. This happened time and again when we first went to Indy. We made the mistake of trying to change the car for the driver to go faster, but now we park the car and wait until the driver or the time of day comes right. . . .'

Setting up a time schedule for race day is important so that the mechanics and the drivers know exactly when and where they will be required. In general Teddy makes out a list for the chief mechanic which tells him what time practice is, what time they have to be at the track, and what time the cars have to be ready to go on the grid. The night before a work list is prepared and given to the chief mechanic which details all the items that have to be checked or altered on the cars in addition to normal preparation.

These time schedules are an important item that can easily be overlooked. Things like traffic delays on race morning have to be taken into account when working out the movement programme.

Pit equipment for CanAm or Indianapolis racing is more extensive than in European Formula 1 races where a pit stop usually means curtains for the driver's chances anyway. In America the emphasis is on finishing a race at all costs because of the prize-money-only arrangements, but in Europe the financial arrangements are different with a fixed amount of travel expenses paid for each car and driver payments based on his performance driving the previous season. The prize money has been greatly increased under the new 'Geneva' scale down to twentieth place. A pitstop during a 200-mile Grand Prix, then, means that it is seldom worthwhile continuing if the problem takes too long to fix, mainly because of the loss of World championship points.

The pit set-up in America includes a complete body section – nose and tail – for each car, as well as materials to repair damage to the body, a complete set of spare wheels for each car, and quick-lift jacks ready in each pit. Air lines are rigged to power wrenches to speed wheel changes, and spare fuel is kept in churns. Oil cannot be added during a race. The team have developed a pressurized water system so that an overheating car can have water pumped in under pressure during a pit stop without unscrewing the water cap. Tools are laid out ready for use, and the signalling numbers and name boards are set out for quick selection during the race.

Teddy keeps track of his own drivers with two pairs of sixty-second-sweep Heuer stopwatches, stopping one watch and starting the other as the car passes. As well as keeping every lap time for each driver, he can also record the pluses and minuses on cars ahead and behind. 'If I start my watch on zero when Denny goes by,' says Teddy, describing a hypothetical situation, 'I can wait for Jackie Stewart to go by and by glancing at the watch I can tell within a tenth or two that he is seven seconds behind Denny. Or if someone is ahead of Denny and he goes past at a minute and fifteen seconds on my watch and Denny's lap time is one minute twenty, I know that he is five seconds ahead of Denny. On every lap I note Denny's time, his plus and his minus, and his position.'

Teddy does not keep a lap chart and he does not feel that one is important in relatively short 200-mile 'sprints' which most of the CanAm and Grand Prix races are.

'In a long distance race where there could be dramatic drop-outs and you may need to know whether you are seven laps behind or two in front, a lap chart would be very important, but in a short race as long as you know the laps your driver has run and the number of laps the leader has run, really it's up to the driver because he's going as hard as he can. Once in a while a situation where it rains and you're in and out of the pits, a lap chart would be useful, but generally speaking we don't bother because you don't have enough advantage on your competitors to take it very easy, and they don't have enough advantage on you so that they can take it easy. The races aren't really long enough to play tactics. Keeping a lap chart at Indy is a mammoth task – it's one of those races where you go out and run as hard and fast as you can for the 500 miles and then find out where you are officially placed afterwards!'

12 The Commercial Importance of Racing in America

CanAm racing established the McLaren team, and it made Bruce a better-known personality in America than he was in England or in Europe. From his early races with Cooper Monacos at Laguna Seca and Riverside he became aware of the tremendous potential of American sports car racing and he wanted Cooper to become more involved, but they preferred to make their commitment in Grand Prix racing and this was one of the reasons that prompted Bruce to start up his own team.

Success in the American races brought much-needed finance to the small team, and it also helped to build a reputation that was extremely useful when Bruce and Teddy Mayer went searching for sponsors. Teddy regards CanAm and Indianapolis racing as being much more important to the survival of the team than European Grand Prix racing.

'The reason for this is economic as much as anything. Most of our sponsorship comes from America, and generally speaking the Americans don't know very much about Formula 1. It gets less publicity in the States than CanAm and far less coverage than Indy. Therefore if you do well in front of your sponsors in CanAm racing or at Indy, you're doing well as far as they're concerned – they probably wouldn't be too worried if we didn't run in Formula 1 at all. In fact we divide our racing into three more or less equal parts – CanAm, Indy and Formula 1 – they all cost about the same to take part in, and all bring in about the same amount of money, so we can't afford to drop Formula 1 and only run in the States.'

Initially, the McLaren team ran with Firestone but later

switched to Goodyear and they have been with them ever since. Other major sponsors are Reynolds Aluminium and the Gulf Oil Corporation.

It has always been McLaren team policy to restrict the number of sponsors and the number of advertising decals on the cars, so that the major sponsors with a large investment in the team are assured of getting maximum exposure on the racing car rather than being swamped with a mass of smaller trade decals. In some cases this means that the team lose on contingency monies posted for the winner, but in the long run they profit because their efforts at exclusivity are appreciated by the sponsoring companies.

Teddy feels that a company like Goodyear, the largest tyre company in the world, goes racing because the performance image, or the association with high performance, differentiates their product from other similar products in the eyes of the public.

'To me, this is the biggest value that they get from going racing. They get a good deal of publicity from it, but the publicity is keyed to the theory that because that company is associated with successful high performance products, they have the ability and the know-how to make production goods that are better, goods that have higher performance characteristics than those of other similar companies which don't and are not associated with racing and with high performance success.'

Long term, this involvement in racing could mean better Goodyear tyres for the everyday motorist. 'I think it is specious to argue that development in racing leads to development in production vehicles or in any production item. When I say racing, I don't mean saloon-car racing or rallying or anything of that nature because I think there is a definite tie-in there – you find things that can improve your reliability or performance, but to say that a Formula 1 tyre bears relationship to the tyre on a Cadillac is generally speaking pretty far-fetched. There have been instances where theories worked out in Grand Prix racing can be applied, but it's very much on a long-term basis and certainly not a direct application of racing principles.

'I have been speaking specifically of Goodyear here, but the benefit to Gulf or Reynolds is also mainly through their association with high performance success. It's a means of getting publicity and creating an image in the public eye, rather than any great direct engineering benefit.'

Bruce had the ideal sort of personality for working with sponsoring companies, and he worked hard to give good value for the financial support that the company was giving to the team. This is a relatively new area for European drivers and not many have the flair for promoting a sponsor. Stirling Moss was the first of the real professional drivers in England and he now hosts the Johnson Wax sponsorship of the CanAm series. Jackie Stewart recently signed with Goodyear to run in the CanAm series with a Lola and he regards the American races as being most important for the furthering of his career.

'To give a sponsor good value for his money requires considerable effort,' says Mayer. 'It means that you've got to have time to do commercials and advertising shots with his public relations company for magazines, newspapers and television; you've got to mention him in interviews. This was another of the reason why we decided to limit the number of sponsoring companies we could accept. You have to work to promote the image of the sponsor and in the time you have available it's impossible to project the image of more than a strictly limited number of companies. Certainly you can't promote two companies that sell the same product or even operate in similar fields.'

When the team signed with Goodyear in 1967 they were told that the tyre company regarded the sponsorship as an investment in a future Indianapolis programme, but in fact it was 1970 before a McLaren ran at the 'brickyard'. When the M15 cars were being built to take the turbo-charged Offenhauser Bruce talked enthusiastically about their plans and when they decided to take on the American 'establishment'. 'We were at Mosport listening to a radio broadcast of the 1969 race and when Denny was up in second place and then dropped out, we

k ind of looked ateach other and said, "To hell with it, let's have
a go and build a car for him".' As it turned out Denny was not
able to drive in the 500 because of his accident in practice, and
Chris Amon, the other scheduled driver of the all-Kiwi assault
on Indy, also decided not to drive there, so the cars started with
the Americans, Peter Revson and Carl Williams, driving.

For 1971 the McLaren team returned to Indianapolis with a
completely revised programme and a new pair of cars. They
learnt a lot from their year as a 'rooky team' in 1970.

'We ran a lot too much and we ran at the wrong times,' says
Teddy, outlining plans for Indianapolis the second time around.
'We put a lot of emphasis on running as much as possible to find
out as much as we could about the track, starting early every
morning and running all day. Because of the long start-up
procedure with the Offy, this meant that the mechanics had to
be at the track at about 6am every morning and worked late at
night, and this pretty much wore them out. I don't think that
this was necessary, and we certainly did a lot of redundant
running. We were changing things on the car when in fact it
was the track or the driver's mood that had changed.

'The track conditions alter a great deal between the time the
track opens at 9am, noon and 6pm when the track closes. This
means that if you're running all day, you have to keep changing
the car to compensate for the change in track conditions, so
you're not really proving anything. The race is run between 11am
and 2pm so we will be doing most of our running during this
period of the day and not trying to be on the track all the time.'

Gordon Coppuck, the designer, feels there was no point in
being on the track on May 1 with their three cars running nose
to tail because, although they made an impressive sight for a
new team, all they really did was to confuse themselves. 'The
circuit was so dirty from the winter that the drivers could not
get a competitive time in anyway and all we did was mess the
car around trying to go as quick as we had done when we were
testing in November. Next time we'll let someone else run all
the dust off the track. We really got a shock when we found that

we couldn't go quicker than 164mph on those first few days in May, but we should have realized that not many of the front chargers like Foyt and Ruby were there that early – they turned up two or three days later when the track was cleaner, but by that time we had messed our car up.'

Indianapolis was a track that never really appealed to Bruce. He couldn't get to grips with having to average over 160mph in such a confined space with all the engineering effort being aimed at making a car go through four fast left-handers. He knew there was a special science involved in that $2\frac{1}{2}$-mile track, but until he went there during the November testing and later during the month of May, he never realized just how complex that science was.

'Indy is a whole new ball game,' he said in his *Autosport* column after the November tests with the new car. 'First of all, you don't run much below 160mph and most of the time you are nearer 200mph. In Grand Prix racing or CanAm it's the other way round – you're not much over 160mph and this is the first thing you notice.

'We hadn't been to Indy before and we didn't know much about it, but I was much more interested in finding out why and how a car is fast at Indianapolis for myself, rather than just copying all the trick things that people had developed over the years. I drove the car initially myself but then I realized that my lack of experience was going to hurt just a little. It takes quite a long time to go really fast there. Make no mistake, it's a lot more than just four left-hand corners. There's a very definite art in getting through those high-speed turns correctly. You have to run a very precise line and pattern – at least I think so – to go fast . . .'

Denny Hulme lapped at 168mph during these tests and Bruce got up to 165mph and they left the Indianapolis track very pleased with their efforts. In fact Bruce went faster in November than Chris was ever able to run in May. Chris was probably somewhat un-nerved by Denny's fire, and like Bruce, he was just a little unsure of what he was doing there anyway. This made it difficult for the team. With Denny driving they knew they were working with someone who had proven himself to be competitive in this special sphere of racing, and they were able to alter the car accordingly, to his suggestions. Gordon summed it up well. 'We always had a suspicion that if Denny had been able to drive he could have run quick enough to win the race, but we weren't sure whether the others were able to.'

Tyler likened their problem to trying to sort out a Formula 1 car with a driver who could not tell them whether it was over-steering or understeering!

Bruce had been anxious to treat Indy as just another race, but Denny, who had been subjected to the sort of 'magic' at Indy, scoffed that it was not 'just another race' if you had to design special shock absorbers for it! After the November tests Bruce came away saying he had never been so excited about one race before.

'We went there not knowing whether our competitors were super sophisticated or very naïve. When we got there we found that there were really two classes and we were just a little surprised that there was such a depth of good equipment – we had expected to see more rubbish and less of the good quality cars,' said Gordon. He and Bruce were pleased at the stir the new McLarens caused in Gasoline Alley, and they were delighted when the Indiana section of the Society of Automobile Engineers presented Bruce with a plaque in recognition of his contribution towards progress at Indy.

Coming home in the plane Bruce and Gordon sat together and went carefully through what they had just gathered in the way of new ideas at the Speedway, discussing ways in which these ideas could be incorporated in a McLaren for 1971. 'We decided that we hadn't seen the concept of our new car and that we would have to investigate several basic shapes before coming to a decision. We wondered whether a wedge would be better, or a slim pencil shape, or a fat car. The M15 was what we called a "fat car". It was 45 inches wide whereas our current Formula 1 car was only 26 inches wide.'

The new Indianapolis McLaren M16 will be a wedge. The car that influenced this shape was, in fact, not an Indy car but the Formula 1 Lotus 72 which admittedly gained its shape from the 4-wheel drive Lotus Indy cars. The McLaren will have a chisel nose with the radiators mounted at the side. The 1971 car will keep the turbo-charged Offenhauser and the McLaren link system in the rear suspension, but the front suspension geometry, the wheelbase and the fuel system will all be altered.

The Indianapolis project grew out of the lessons learned in CanAm racing and the M15 was very much a single-seater version of the CanAm car, even using the same suspension uprights. The McLaren team is regarded as being super-dominant in CanAm, but they had to serve a tough apprentice-ship. The Zerex-Olds won first time out at Mosport in 1964 and the first McLaren was a success but although the cars were fast they were dogged by trifling troubles that kept Bruce from the winner's circle time after time. In 1966 when the CanAm series started the Lola T70 Mk2 won five of the six races and John Surtees was champion with three wins at Ste Jovite, Riverside and Las Vegas. Bruce's score was two seconds and two thirds, and he took third in the Championship behind Surtees and Donohue. His take-home pay that year was $22,560. It had been a bad year with the collapse of the Grand Prix effort with the 4-cam Ford engine to contend with as well. With the McLaren M6A for 1967 and Denis Hulme as hired gun, the team fortunes changed. Denny won the three openers, Bruce won Laguna Seca and Riverside and also took the title along with $62,300 and Denny was runner-up with $40,000. In 1968 it was Hulme's turn for the title and the total team pay for the Series was $163,030. In 1969 the Series had grown to eleven races and the orange McLarens rumbled home to win every time, for Bruce's second CanAm crown. The tragic 1970 CanAm series started in the shadow of Bruce's death while testing the latest of the McLaren CanAm cars – the finned Batmobile M8D – but Denny carried the flag to win the Championship and a personal total of $162,202.

These sort of winnings sound great until you rack up the crippling costs of mounting such a racing offensive, leaving nothing to chance. Mayer maintains the costs were not covered until after mid-season in 1969 when they were winning everything in sight. Sponsorship contracts are vital to the McLaren team, and it is this lack of sponsorship that has kept the other major European teams out of the Series.

Phil Kerr says that sponsors always receive value in return from the team. 'It was always a good two-way trade. There were always reciprocal benefits. I don't think Bruce ever knowingly would have made an association with other people or companies where he couldn't or wouldn't keep his part of the bargain. Every effort was made to give the fullest possible value, and in terms of reward the sponsoring companies did very well. There was good publicity from the association with the winning team, and there were also technical benefits because Bruce very frequently became involved with the competition department or the research or technical divisions of the companies and there would be an interchange of information. He could seek information from these people, but would willingly provide information on what he had found applying their products or ideas to his racing cars.'

Typical of this information interchange was the relationship with Harry Macklin in the Automotive Division of Reynolds Aluminium at Richmond in Virginia. Macklin had been working with his development team for twelve years perfecting an all-aluminium engine block which dispensed with cast iron cylinder sleeves and he was well advanced with the 390 alloy block for the engine to power the new Chevrolet Vega when the contract was signed with McLaren Racing. The contract would obviously have a publicity rub-off with Reynolds products throughout their range from Reynolds foil wrap, through to their ideas for building all-aluminium car bodies that could be reclaimed like aluminium beer cans, but Bruce was obviously more interested in the automotive engine developments. Macklin and McLaren discussed building a 390 alloy version of the CanAm Chevrolet engine and during 1969 Bruce was excitedly whispering about progress on this new power unit. In fact, it never ran in a racing car until late in the 1970 season, and at Laguna Seca Denny won the race using the new Reynolds engine. Back in Richmond Macklin was already making plans to reduce the size of the water jackets (the all-aluminium block dissipates heat better without the iron liners) and increase the capacity of the engine up to what he reckoned to be a safe limit of 525 cu. in. – 8.6 litres.

In the five seasons since the CanAm series started there have been 39 races, and 37 of these were won by Chevrolet engines! Underlining the McLaren dominance in recent years – remember they won nothing in 1966 – McLaren cars have won 31 times against six wins for Lola, and one each for Chaparral and Porsche. Denny Hulme, two-time Champion, is top winner for the Series with seventeen J-Wax medals, Bruce won nine and then came John Surtees with four, Dan Gurney with three, Mark Donohue with two, and a win apiece for Phil Hill, John Cannon, Peter Gethin and Tony Dean.

Ken Tyrrell, Jackie Stewart's entrant in Formula 1, maintained that he was not impressed so much by the string of McLaren victories in CanAm racing as by the fact that the cars were always around at the finish of the race. 'If you compared our record of finishes in Formula 1 with McLaren in CanAm, it wouldn't look too bright . . . you can't win if you don't finish.'

The secret of the McLaren success was reliability built from sound engineering. 'Our basic design is good,' Bruce said while the finishing touches were being put to the new CanAm cars for 1970. 'Our sports cars came from our original tube-frame cars which came from Coopers. Since then we have put in a tremendous amount of development and improvement every year. If someone wants to compete with us, they can copy what we've got, but they will lack the background of research and experiment that taught us the lessons we built into our new cars. Other people can copy, but they will be doing it blindly and in doing that they can make a mistake.

'I often say to people in our drawing office and to the mechanics and engineers, "Copy if you understand exactly why, but don't just copy blindly because the moment you do that, you're in terrible trouble". You have to find out *why* something is done that way, do an experiment to find out why, and *then* you can copy something. In short, this is just plain good engineering. And this is why our cars are so good – they're well engineered.'

13 Trojan Production and Special McLaren Projects

'When we planned the original McLaren, it was going to be just that. A special car built by my pocket-sized team, around me, and for me. The idea was for us to win races. The prototype McLaren was almost a freehand affair and when we built it in November 1964 we speculated on the possibilities of handling production ourselves, figuring on a limited line of six, but when we looked at delivery schedules and production costs on the car we were building, we shuddered and decided there were enough problems and costs involved in running one team car without buying a customer's woes when we sold a production model.' Bruce McLaren was talking about the first year of his team's existence when production was a pipe-dream of the immediate future.

When the M1A was so successful there were several enquiries for copy-cars but after consideration Bruce decided against going into production even on a limited basis. That was when Frank Nichols of Elva Cars came round to the factory in Feltham with a proposition to handle production of 'customer' McLarens. Elva were at this stage building small-capacity sports-racing cars at their factory at Rye on the Sussex coast.

The Lambretta-Trojan group rescued Nichols' Elva company, re-forming it as Elva Cars (1961) Ltd after it had gone into liquidation, and at Nichols' suggestion a deal was arranged between Peter Agg, managing director of Lambretta-Trojan, and McLaren Racing, whereby the Elva company at Rye would build production McLaren sports cars for sale as McLaren-Elvas.

The agreement was signed on November 21, 1964, and work started immediately to have the first McLaren-Elva ready for the Racing Car Show in January.

There were twenty-four M1A McLaren-Elvas sold and they were marketed in the US as the Mark 2. There were difficulties surrounding the first run of production cars, firstly because the prototype was being raced in America at the time of the initial discussions and then most of the McLaren team – which numbered six at the time – went out to the Tasman series during January and February with the two Coopers for Bruce and Phil Hill. Another problem was that there were no manufacturing drawings. It was one thing for the racing team to build a one-off car as they went along, but quite another to set up a manufacturing process for a run of several cars.

'When you build a prototype car,' said Bruce, 'the most sensible method is to settle upon the suspension geometry you want first. Then the basic chassis structure is drawn to accommodate that geometry. Most of all the bits and pieces – roll bars, steering column mounts, battery mounts, brake lines, switches, instruments, body fasteners, etc. ad nauseam, are put into the chassis wherever your experience tells you they will fit and work. To lay all that out in three dimensions on the drawing board would take the best part of a year and the design would be obsolete by the time it got to the track. But these drawings have to be made in order to build a series of cars and this was the first snag we encountered. We had problems getting wheels designed and cast in time, and then came drama with the bodies. The prototype had an aluminium body built in a back alley by two old-timers in the panel-beating game in under three weeks, and this body was to be used as a mould for the production bodies which were to be in fibreglass to cut down costs.'

Because Bruce was on the Tasman series at the time the moulds were made he was not able to pass judgment and when he returned to England he found that the bodies were not quite to his liking, but by then it was too late.

'Building a racing car is not the simplest task you can undertake and building a series of them just multiplies the difficulties by the number of cars you intend making . . .'

The M1A was designed specifically for the Oldsmobile engine, although customers for the first cars tried fitting Chevrolet and Ford engines with varying degrees of success. The M1B (or the Mk 2 as it was known in America) catered for other engines and during 1965 and 1966 Trojan built twenty-eight of these cars. The M1B and M1C (known as the Mk 3) were improvements and revisions on the spaceframe theme of the original prototype M1A, with modifications being passed on from the current cars raced by the McLaren team. Trojan built twenty-five M1C McLarens for a total of seventy-seven cars following the basic lines laid down by Bruce for the M1A.

In 1967 the new monocoque M6A sports car swept all before it in the CanAm series and for 1968 Trojan built a productionized version called the M6B and sold twenty-six. In 1969 an attempt was made to homologate a GT version of the M6 CanAm car for long-distance racing, but despite technically meeting the FIA requirements, it was not accepted as a Group 4 car and only four M6GTs were built. David Prophet raced one in England, Bruce had one as a development vehicle for a possible McLaren road car, one was shipped to a customer in America, and a fourth was built by Trojan for their own display purposes. Trojan still talk of producing a road car and Peter Agg reckons that with a 'cooking' V8 engine he could produce a road-going McLaren GT for around £6,500 including taxes in England.

The attractive little M4 Formula 2 monocoque designed by Robin Herd at the beginning of 1967 was put into production by Trojan later that year and sold as a chassis for Formula 2, 3, or American Formula B racing, but lack of time for development made it one of the least successful McLaren cars.

The M12 customer car for 1969 used an M6-type chassis with a body along the lines of the M8A and fourteen of these were built. The M8C was a further refinement of the M6/M12 line, differing from the M8A works car in that pontoons behind the rear bulkhead were provided to ease the installation of engines other than the aluminium Chevrolet that was stressed in the construction of the works M8A and M8B. Eight M8Cs were sold in 1970, and for 1971 the production model will be the M8E which is a copy of the original M8 with the monocoque ending abruptly behind the cockpit. Customers can order the M8E with M8C-type pontoons to aid engine mounting if they do not wish to use the engine as a stress-bearing member.

During 1970 a prototype known as the M8E was built and tested by Denny Hulme at Goodwood and was, in fact, a reversion to the narrower track and body of the M8B but with a low wing mounted to a frame over the transmission instead of the high wing of the M8B or the fins and wing of the M8D. This car was never raced because the monocoque tub was needed as a spare to replace the tub in Denny Hulme's car which was damaged in an accident at the Road Atlanta race in September.

An important project for Trojan was the line of single-seater M10 cars for the 5-litre Formula 5,000 in England, Formula A in America and the Tasman series. In 1969 and 1970 Peter Gethin won the Formula 5,000 championship in England using an M10A and an M10B. John Cannon won the Formula A title with an M10B in America in 1970, and that season in England Sir Nicholas Williamson won the British Hillclimb championship with an M10B. Patsy Burt also won the British Sprint championship in 1970 with her M3A. Trojan sold twenty M10As and twenty-two M10Bs.

The McLaren/Trojan alliance has resulted in a peculiarly happy marriage for both companies, since Trojan benefit by the specialist racing experience of the works and team modifications can be passed on to the production models when significant improvements have been made in the works cars. The McLaren team gets the enormous advantage of being free of ninety per cent of the worries normally associated with customer production and they can also take advantage of the Trojan stocks of components when building up prototype cars.

New production cars are usually the result of prototype

'guinea-pig' cars being built at Colnbrook, tested until they are competitive and then handed over to Trojan to produce replicas.

Peter James Agg, who is 41, is a businessman to the tips of his handlebar moustaches and he pushes eagerly ahead with new developments in his group of companies. On the road he drives a Bentley and an Iso Grifo and as a hobby he has a front-wheel-drive Derby Maserati historic racing car. Bruce wondered at first whether his specialized racing team would be able to work side by side with this old-school-tie sort of figure but he soon discovered that Agg's approach was strictly British executive and businesslike.

The Lambretta-Trojan group of companies includes the Lambretta scooter concession for Great Britain and they market around 10,000 of these scooters each year. Agg personally owns Suzuki (Great Britain) Limited and has handed the running of the company over to Lambretta. Next to Honda, Agg's Suzuki operation is the largest distributor of motorcycles in the country, selling around 10,000 a year. Included in the group is the national distributorship for Homelite chain saws and 20,000 of these are sold annually. Agg also has the agency for the Italian Iso cars but the sleek Grifo GT, costing around £8,500 in 7-litre form, seems over-priced on the British market.

The total staff of the group numbers around 270 and this includes a property company with a complete construction crew that built the offices and factories on the Lambretta-Trojan fifteen-acre estate at Purley.

The racing division is housed at present in a 10,000 square foot factory but Agg talks of moving to another factory on the estate with an area of 27,000 square feet and they will be branching out into the engine-building side of racing. In 1970 Frank Gardner's Formula 5,000 Lola was extremely competitive using a Chevrolet engine built by Louis Morand in Switzerland and Agg has arranged to handle sales of this engine in England. They will build 5-litre engines for Formula A/5,000 and 7-litre units for CanAm and the Group 7 Inter-Series which is increasing in popularity in Europe and bringing CanAm cars into Europe.

Agg and his works director John Bennett investigated the possibilities of building light aircraft since the construction process is not too dissimilar to that of the monocoque racing cars but they found that the market for aircraft in Great Britain was too limited.

In the Suzuki workshops ideas from the McLaren car-building construction have been borrowed in the form of an aluminium monocoque for a trials bike weighing 30lb. less than the normal tube frame, and much stronger.

Some of the McLaren car-building staff have moved to Trojan from Colnbrook to help with the liaison between the racing team and the customer production, and Bill Meace, who ran production with the old Elva company (the name has been dropped in favour of the Trojan label on the cars now) works closely with Harry Pearce at Colnbrook.

The Automatic McLaren

Jim Hall's Chaparrals were hard cars to beat in 1964 and Bruce put a lot of credit for their pace down to the fact that Hall was using a form of automatic transmission. To try and counter this advantage, Bruce talked with Tony Rolt at Harry Ferguson Research and a special Ferguson torque converter with a 2-speed gearbox behind it was adapted to fit the M1A sports car in 1965. In the initial testing at Oulton Park Chris Amon took half a second off the lap record set the year before by Jim Clark in a Formula 1 Lotus.

This performance prompted Bruce to enter the automatic car for the Tourist Trophy at Oulton Park in May, but the problems that manifested themselves that weekend spelt the end of the Ferguson project. A seal in the torque converter shifted after Bruce had done seven laps in the first practice session and the mechanics stripped the unit to mend it. After only one lap in the second practice a con-rod broke in the engine and with only eight laps of practice done Bruce had to settle for second fastest time behind John Surtees in the Lola and the crew worked all night to install a new engine.

There was a special technique in making a grid start with the car because the transmission had a tendency to 'creep' and the driver had to sit on the grid with his left foot hard on the brake, his right foot building up revs with the accelerator and the car trying to overcome the brakes and crawl forward!

Bruce took the lead in the TT when Surtees' Lola's steering failed after a couple of laps, but after ten laps fluid started leaking from the torque converter again and Bruce stopped. Tyler and the other mechanics stripped the still-secret unit on the pit bench with the cars thundering past a few feet away and had the transmission repaired and rebuilt in time for the start of the second heat. Bruce stormed off the back of the grid and was through on the tail of Jim Clark in the Lotus 30, setting a new track record of 100.4mph in the process before the oil pressure started to drop and he pitted before the engine destroyed itself again.

After an investigation of the problems they had suffered at the TT and during testing they discovered that the operation of the torque converter kept the engine working too low in the rev range and this was causing pre-ignition, and blowing the engines.

The automatic McLaren had proved itself to be a record-breaker, but the team were not convinced that the mechanical problems associated with the transmission were worth solving, and it seemed likely that they would be better rewarded putting the same effort into further development on the sports car using a conventional transmission.

The Ford GTX

Bruce, Richie Ginther and Roy Salvadori were the first test drivers hired by Ford for development work on the GT40s and Bruce and Phil Hill drove a GT40 in its first race at the Nurburgring 1,000 Km in 1964. The car dropped out of second place when a weld failed in the rear suspension. Bruce was impressed with the potential of the Ford GTs and he worked in well with Yorkshireman Roy Lunn who had designed the front-wheel-drive Cardinal with an advanced design crew at Dearborn before the car was handed over to Ford in Germany to become the Taunus 26M. Lunn was also responsible for the little 1.7 litre mid-engined open two-seater that was known as Mustang 1, a vehicle to test public reaction to a sports car from Ford. Later Lunn worked with Eric Broadley on the development of the first GT40s which were closely based on the Lola GT Eric had built in 1963.

Towards the end of the 1964 season Lunn and McLaren discussed the chances of the McLaren team building up a special open version of the GT40 to see if it had potential as a CanAm type sports car. This was a suitable arrangement for the growing McLaren team because, as Teddy Mayer said later, Ford contracts to do anything at that time were extremely lucrative. From the Ford point of view the McLaren team were ideally suited to build a big sports car because of their experience in this field, and their liaison with Bruce was already well established.

The result was that the McLaren team was given a prototype GT40 (chassis number GT40/110) with a 7-litre engine and the go-ahead to start the development project. Gary Knutson was put in charge of the car that was known as the GTX, converting the GT into an open car and radically altering the structure. The GTX emerged much lighter than the GT40 with a single-sheet aluminium monocoque in place of the GT40's 23-gauge sheet steel hull. One of Ford's main objects in handing the GTX project over to the McLaren team was to have the work done quickly and efficiently and to decide whether to pursue the aluminium monocoque or go towards the new honeycomb material for the new cars they were developing.

Chris Amon raced the GTX at Mosport, Riverside and Nassau, but finished only once. He was fifth at Riverside. At the end of the season the GTX stayed in America and was altered to take a new nose with the larger screen required by the regulations for long-distance races. It was entered in the Sebring twelve-hour race in 1966 and it won, driven by Ken

Miles and Lloyd Ruby. After that race the car was scrapped, but Ford had benefited from the development of the GTX at Feltham – the new Mark 4 Ford 7-litre cars used the honeycomb sheet in their monocoque tubs.

Bruce and Mario Andretti won the 1967 Sebring race in the first of the Mk 4 Fords (Bruce had won at Le Mans in a Mk 2) and the Gurney/Foyt Mk 4 won at Le Mans the same year.

Alfa Romeo Engines in Formula 1
At the beginning of 1970 an arrangement was made with Auto Delta (the factory-owned Alfa Romeo racing team) whereby the McLaren team would supply a Formula 1 chassis to be fitted with the T33 3-litre Alfa Romeo V8 and the car would be driven by Andrea de Adamich.

The engine was basically a sports car unit originally built as a 2-litre in 1967 and developed to the point where it gave around 410 horsepower in Formula 1 trim. One of the problems with the installation of the Alfa Romeo engine in the M7 chassis was that a mounting had to be arranged for the alternator which is not integral with the engine as it is on the Ford-Cosworth V8. This M7 received a D suffix to differentiate it from the Ford-engined works M7Cs.

The horsepower did not match the Ford but it was felt that with the resources of the Alfa Romeo company behind Auto Delta, a competitive engine could be built if the Formula 1 venture was at all successful. It was also a team hedge against the rash of unreliability suffered during the 1970 season with the Ford engines as Cosworth struggled to look after seventy units in use as well as track down a problem with harmonic balancing.

Later in the season de Adamich drove a new M14 McLaren with the Alfa Romeo engine fitted and Giovanni Marelli, a young Ferrari racing engineer, was hired to look after the engine but the car continued to be plagued with problems relating to engine performance and reliability and at the end of the season the alliance between the Italian factory and the McLaren team was dissolved.

Postscript

Before the South African Grand Prix in March 1970 Bruce hired an air-conditioned Ford Fairlane and drove Patty, Amanda, my wife Sandra and me, up to the Kruger Park game reserve for five days of relaxation cruising along the dusty roads and watching the wild animals in their natural surroundings. The fact that Bruce collected us from the Johannesburg airport, loaded our cases in the trunk, tossed his coat in on top and then slammed the lid just as he remembered the car keys were in the coat pocket served to indicate that five days of McLaren hilarity lay ahead. Away from the pressures of the factory Bruce liked nothing better than to enjoy himself doing new things or flopping about in a swimming pool. The project for that week was to teach Amanda to swim. His enthusiasm was infectious and Amanda was soon trying a few solo strokes.

At the end of that week Bruce drove the new M14A at Kyalami and was overhauling Jackie Stewart's March when the engine blew. Denny finished second behind Jack's new Brabham. At Jarama Bruce was second, but at Monaco he clipped the chicane and was out with damaged suspension after twenty laps. Then he was jet-hopping back to Indianapolis for the qualifying weekends.

Before he left Monaco he sat around the pool at the Metropole Hotel and talked about his plans. He was getting slightly disenchanted with Grand Prix racing, he said, and he went on to rationalize the thinking behind his talk of phasing himself out of Formula 1.

'I consider that I could be a good racing driver or a good engineer. I feel I could be a better racing driver than I am and I could be a better engineer than I am, but I could be a better engineer than a racing driver and the company is going to be dependent on its cars and on its engineering more than on its drivers.'

Bruce was by no means selling himself short as a driver, though. At the end of the previous season he had won the British Racing Drivers' Club Gold Star for most points scored during 1969, and his total pipped the World Champion, Jackie Stewart.

When he had time to appreciate it, Bruce was enjoying life in a manner that he thoroughly deserved. He had moved into a large modern home in a private park, and in the lounge a selection of his trophies reminded him of his progress. Trophy shelves flanked the chimney breast. There was the International Trophy for winning the hectic duel with John Surtees at Silverstone in 1965 with the sports car. Behind it stood a model of a 158 Alfa Romeo with the left front wheel propped beside it. A silver salver with a McLaren badge inset recorded five years of successful association with Trojan building the production McLarens. A colour photograph of Piers and Sally Courage and their family looked over three silver CanAm medals and the replica of the Tasman Cup that Bruce won in 1964.

On a shelf below was a silver plate won at Solitude in 1961 with the Formula 1 Cooper, a photograph beside it showed Bruce hooting with laughter at some joke as he hauled his Nomex mask off at Brands Hatch in the pits, and there were the Auto World models of the M8A and the winged M8B standing with five gold CanAm medals and a silver cup from winning a Formula Vee race at Nassau. On the other side of the chimney was the 1968 Ferodo Trophy closely watched by a photograph of Amanda as a baby, two Martini gold medals, and the B.R.D.C. Gold Star. In pride of place was the Segrave Trophy – awarded for the most outstanding technical achievement by a British subject on land or sea or in the air – and at the top of the plaque were the words 'Imagination, Courage, Initiative'.

It had been awarded to the right man. The only pity was that he never lived to receive it.

When the numbing shock of Bruce's death had been replaced by a disbelief that such a thing could have happened, Teddy, Phil, Tyler and Denny pushed ahead with the team's programme for 1970. They lacked their late leader's drive and enthusiasm, but they were determined to keep going 'for Bruce'.

Denny's burned hands were still extremely painful but he spurred recovery to drive one of the M8Ds in the first CanAm race at Mosport on June 14. Dan Gurney had been signed to take Bruce's place and he carried the Kiwi banner to wins in the first two races. Denny was third at Mosport and then gave the Dutch GP at Zandvoort a miss while he waited for his hands to heal properly. The team had withdrawn their entries from the Belgian Grand Prix as a mark of respect to Bruce, and for Zandvoort Dan Gurney and Peter Gethin were driving with Denny on hand to offer expert advice.

Denny made his comeback with a win in the Watkins Glen CanAm race after engine troubles had delayed Gurney. Problems over a sponsorship clash meant that Dan was replaced in the CanAm team by Gethin who flew out with Denny in time for the Edmonton race. Denny made it three in a row with Edmonton and Mid-Ohio following his Glen victory. Gethin had a controversial win in the Road America race when Denny was penalised for allegedly being push-started after a spin. Peter had waited for his team leader to catch up and take the flag ahead of him, but the officials credited Denny only with the laps done before his spin and he was relegated to fifteenth place.

Both M8Ds were damaged in race accidents at Road Atlanta and Tony Dean won in the 3-litre 908 Porsche. It was the first time any car but a McLaren had won a CanAm race since John Surtees won with his Lola at the end of the 1967 season in Las Vegas!

Denny rounded off the 1970 season with wins at Donnybrooke, Laguna Seca and Riverside and won the Championship with 132 points, nearly double the score of second man Lothar Motschenbacher with 65 points, in his production McLaren

M12. Peter Gethin finished third on final standings after his engine blew up at Riverside and ruined his chances of overhauling Lothar's score. It was the first time in four years that Team McLaren had missed their traditional 1--2 finish in the championship.

It had been a ragged season in Formula 1 for the McLaren team with Bruce's death, Denny's accident at Indianapolis and then Gurney and Gethin driving only part of the season. Denny's best result was his second place in South Africa with thirds in the British, German and Mexican Grands Prix in the M14A.

For 1971 Peter Gethin will team again with Hulme in Formula 1 with new M19A Ford-engined cars, but Peter Revson will join Team McLaren in America driving the second CanAm McLaren and the second McLaren M16A wedge in the big 500-mile races at Indianapolis, Ontario and Pocono.

Appendix
McLaren Cars - 1965-70

M1A The original McLaren-built Group 7 car was a simple
spaceframe design powered by a light and compact Oldsmobile
V8 engine. The type was put into production as the McLaren-
Elva Mark 1 and versions appeared with 4.7 litre Ford V8
power in addition to the standard 4.5 litre Olds unit. A total of
24 were built and met with some success, although it soon
became apparent that the Olds engine was just too small for the
class.

CHASSIS Large diameter round and square tubular frame
with light alloy sheet riveted and bonded to it, forming stressed
undertray and bulkheads.

SUSPENSION Independent -- unequal length wide-based
wishbones, anti-roll bar and adjustable coil-spring dampers at
front. Trailing radius arms with single top links, reversed lower
wishbones, anti-roll bar and adjustable coil-spring dampers at
rear.

BRAKES Dual circuit Girling discs all round.

BODY Four-section polyester resin moulded body with integral brakes and radiator ducting and side sections housing twin
fuel tanks.

ENGINE Traco Oldsmobile 4.5 litre V8 as standard mated to
a Hewland LG four-speed gearbox. At least one 4.7 Ford-
powered example also appeared.

DIMENSIONS Wheelbase, 91 inches; Front track, 51 inches;
Rear track, 51 inches.

M1B This Group 7 sports-racing car was the 1966 development of the original M1A design. Rebuilt with a new chassis,

new body and many other modifications it was put into production at Elva's Rye factory and sold in the States as the McLaren-Elva Mark 2. Standard Oldsmobile or optional Ford and Chevrolet V8s could be fitted. The works cars driven by McLaren and Amon competed in the first CanAm series run that season, using Chevrolet V8s with Hilborn injection. 28 were made.

CHASSIS Large diameter round and square tubular frame with light alloy sheet riveted and bonded to it forming undertray and bulkheads.

SUSPENSION Independent – unequal length wide-base wishbones with anti-dive characteristics, anti-roll bar and adjustable coil-spring dampers at front. Trailing arms with lower wishbones, single top links, anti-roll bar and adjustable coil-spring dampers at rear. McLaren-Elva cast magnesium wheels 15-inch × 8½-inch front and 15-inch × 11½-inch rear (5.50 and 6.50 × 15 tyres).

BRAKES Dual-circuit Girling discs all round, 12½-inch diameter front and 11½-inch diameter rear.

BODY Four-section polyester resin moulded body with integral brake and radiator ducting and side sections housing twin 25-gallon rubber fuel cells.

ENGINE Traco Oldsmobile 4.5 litre V8 as standard mated via single-plate Schiefer clutch to four-speed Hewland LG gearbox. Hypoid crown-wheel and pinion with limited-slip differential standard in this transmission. Chevrolet and Ford engines and ZF transmission optional equipment.

DIMENSIONS Wheelbase, 91 inches; Front track, 51 inches; Rear track, 51 inches; Overall length, 146 inches; Overall width, 64 inches; Height to top of screen, 31 inches; Weight (less fuel) 1,400lbs distributed 40 per cent/60 per cent front to rear.

M1C While the works ran their first monocoque sports cars in the 1967 CanAm series the Trojan-built customer cars were still space-frame developments of the original design. These

M1C variants, sold as Mark 3s, were generally provided with Chevrolet engines although Oldsmobile and Ford options were still listed. The model was a further improved and developed M1B with a separate spoiler wing at the tail. 25 were built.

CHASSIS Large diameter tubular space-frame with light alloy sheet bonded and riveted to it, forming undertray and bulkheads.

SUSPENSION As for M1B.

BRAKES Dual-circuit Girling discs all round, 12-inch diameter front and 11½-inch diameter rear.

BODY As for M1B

ENGINE As for M1B with Chevrolet V8s as usual equipment and optional four- or five-speed Hewland LG transmissions. ZF transmission still offered.

DIMENSIONS Wheelbase, 90½ inches; Front track, 52 inches; Rear track, 52 inches; Overall length, 146 inches; Overall width, 66 inches; Height to top of screen, 31 inches; Weight (less fuel), 1,300lbs distributed 50 per cent/60 per cent front to rear.

M2A This was an early exercise in producing a Mallite monocoque, and was the team's first single-seater design. It was the work of Robin Herd and he had borrowed Mallite – an aluminium/balsa/aluminium sandwich material – from experience in the aircraft industry. It was light but extremely strong and this one-off car was used as a mobile development rig for a forthcoming Formula 1 car and served Firestone very well as a tyre test vehicle. It used Traco Oldsmobile and Ford V8 engines and gave rise to many rumours of McLaren 'having a Formula 1 car'. In fact the car was never raced, but many lessons learned from its testing performances were incorporated in the M2B.

M2B McLaren Racing's first Formula 1 car, the M2B was another Robin Herd-designed Mallite monocoque. Technically it was a spectacular success, for the chassis was probably the stiffest racing or open car unit ever built with a torsional rigidity approaching 10,000lbs/ft per degree. The 1966 season was the first to be run under 3-litre Formula 1 regs, however, and McLaren chose a de-stroked Indy Ford V8 for his motive power. This unit proved extremely unreliable, suffering from fragile big-end bearings, and was replaced temporarily by an underpowered Serenissima V8 in mid-season. The Ford was resurrected after some development work, but was never a success and the project was shelved at the end of the year. Two chassis were built, but only one raced.

CHASSIS Bath-tub type monocoque formed from Mallite and duralumin panelling formed over mild steel bulkheads.

SUSPENSION Independent – upper rocker arm operating inboard coil-spring dampers with radius arm and lower wishbone at front. Upper transverse link and radius arm, lower reversed wishbone and radius arm with outboard coil-spring dampers at rear. McLaren cast magnesium wheels, 13-inch × 8½-inch fronts and 13-inch × 12-inch rears.

BRAKES Girling discs all round with dual circuits and BR front calipers, AR rears.

BODY Formed by monocoque sides apart from glass-fibre nose cone-cum-cockpit surround, and engine cover used with Ford engine.

ENGINE 3-litre Ford V8 ex-Indianapolis twin-cam engine later replaced temporarily by 3-litre Serenissima V8 based on original ATS design. Mated via a Borg & Beck clutch to five-speed ZF 5DS25 transaxle.

DIMENSIONS Wheelbase, 96 inches; Front track, 59 inches; Rear track, 59 inches.

M3 The team's sports car experiences with big American V8 engines in lightweight tubular chassis during 1965, led to the design and production of this cheap and reliable space-frame single-seater in 1966. It was intended as a Formula Libre, sprint, hill climb and maybe private owner Formula 1 car, priced at £3,000 as a rolling chassis. The engine bay would accept engines from 3- to 6-litres and orders were placed by such notable hillclimb exponents as Harry Zweifel and Miss Patsy Burt. The type proved competitive and tough but only a handful were built before other commitments caused production to cease.

CHASSIS Large-diameter tubular space-frame with steel bulkheads and an aluminium dash panel doubling as a bulkhead in the cockpit area. Chassis tubes carried coolant and an aluminium undertray was bonded and riveted in place to add strength.

SUSPENSION As for M1-series but with optional 15-inch diameter rear wheels.

BRAKES Girling 10 7/16-inch discs all round with AR calipers. Special ½-inch thick discs were available for GP versions or models needing 'to stop from 180mph'.

BODY Polyseter resin moulded panelling to customer preference.

ENGINE To customer preference although engine bay was capable of accepting Oldsmobile, Ford-Cobra and Ford-Indianapolis V8s, 3-litre Repco V8, Maserati V12 and 2.5 or 2.7-litre Coventry Climax 4-cylinder units. Rear bulkheads designed to accept Hewland LG or ZF 5DS25 transaxles.

DIMENSIONS Wheelbase, 96 inches (qualifying for Indy); Front track, 51 inches; Rear track, 52 inches; Overall length, 142 inches; Height to top of screen, 29 inches; Weight (with 5-litre Oldsmobile), 1,100lbs.

M4A For 1967 Robin Herd produced three major designs, for CanAm, Formula 1 and Formula 2. The M4A was a simple bath-tub type monocoque car intended for F2 use and it was raced by Bruce McLaren in about seven Formula 2 events. Some chassis also appeared in Formula 3 guise with little success but Piers Courage raced an F2 M4A in the 1968 Tasman Series and scored the type's only major victory.

CHASSIS Bath-tub monocoque formed from aluminium panelling bonded and riveted to four mild steel bulkheads.

SUSPENSION Single top link with radius arms and lower wishbones, outboard coil-spring dampers and anti-roll bar at front.

Twin radius arms, reversed lower wishbones and single top links with outboard coil-spring dampers at rear. McLaren-Elva cast magnesium wheels all round, 13-inch × 7-inch front and 13-inch × 10-inch rear (5.00 × 13 and 6.25 × 13 tyres).

BRAKES Girling AR calipers on 10½-inch discs all round or alternative Lockheed equivalents.

BODY Formed by monocoque sides plus glass fibre nose cone and cockpit surround.

ENGINE Cosworth-Ford FVA 1,600cc four-cylinder unit mated to five-speed Hewland FT200 transaxle in F2 form.

DIMENSIONS Wheelbase, 90 inches; Front track, 54 inches; Rear track, 54 inches; Overall length, 121 inches; Overall height, 30 inches; Weight (dependent on engine), 830lbs.

M4B The M4B was a production variant of the F2 design, using tuned Lotus-Ford twin cam engines mated to Hewland HD transaxles for American Formula B racing. Another so-called M4B – the subject of this specification – was the interim 1967 Formula 1 car raced by Bruce McLaren. This was a stop-gap measure between the demise of the M2B and the appearance of the new BRM-powered M5A, and had a 3-inch increase in wheelbase to accommodate a 2.1 litre BRM V8 Tasman engine. The car was also fitted with side sponsons to provide extra tankage and was quite successful until written-off in an accident. Meanwhile the true production M4A/B line at Trojan's built 25 cars in 1967/8.

F1 M4B specs as for M4A apart from:

ENGINE 2.1 litre BRM V8 mated to Hewland FT200 trans-axle.

DIMENSIONS Wheelbase, 93 inches; Front track, 54 inches; Rear track, 54 inches; Overall length, 124 inches: Overall height, 30 inches; Weight (with ballast), about 1,120lbs to comply with F1 limit.

M5 The true 1967 McLaren Formula 1 car, the one-off M5 monocoque was a late starter due to delays with its BRM V12 engine. Bruce debuted the car in the Canadian GP and was a strong second until he had to stop to replace a flattened battery. The car was very competitive in its early races, but the V12 was soon outstripped by the Cosworth-Ford V8s and a new car was designed for 1968 to accept the latter units. The M5's last race in works colours was in Hulme's hands at Kyalami, then Jo Bonnier raced the car briefly before putting it on display in his Lausanne, Switzerland, art gallery.

CHASSIS Another aluminium alloy-panelled monocoque formed over mild-steel bulkheads with long pontoons at the rear to support the V12 engine.

SUSPENSION Single top link with radius arm, lower wishbone, anti-roll bar and outboard coil-spring dampers at front. Twin radius arms, single top links, reversed lower wishbones, and outboard coil-spring dampers at rear. Wheels were McLaren cast magnesium, 13-inch × 8½-inch front and 15-inch × 12-inch rear.

BRAKES Lockheed discs and calipers all round.

BODY Formed by monocoque sides apart from glass fibre nose cone and cockpit surround.

ENGINE 3-litre BRM V12 mated via a Borg & Beck clutch to Hewland DG five-speed transaxle.

DIMENSIONS Wheelbase, 96 inches; Front track, 58 inches; Rear track, 58-inches.

M6A Bruce won the 1967 CanAm title with this first monocoque Group 7 car, designed by a kind of committee consisting of himself, Robin Herd, Don Beresford and Tyler Alexander. It was as simple as possible, consisting of single curvatures and square-section tubing wherever they could be used. The M6A was a pure works car and only three were built.

CHASSIS Full monocoque formed from aluminium alloy panelling bonded and riveted to steel bulkheads and carrying two 25-gallon fuel cells in the side pontoons.

SUSPENSION Unequal length upper and lower wishbones, anti-roll bar and coil-spring damper units at front. Upper and lower wishbones with twin radius arms, anti-roll bar and coil-spring dampers at rear. McLaren cast magnesium wheels fitted all round, 15-inch × 8½-inch front and 15-inch × 13¼-inch rear.

BRAKES Girling ventilated discs front and rear, 12-inch diameter, with 16-3-LA calipers and dual hydraulic circuits.

BODY Reinforced polyester resin panelling.

ENGINE 5.9 litre Chevrolet V8 mated to a five-speed Hewland LG transaxle. Engine fitted with Lucas fuel injection.

DIMENSIONS Wheelbase, 93½ inches; Front track, 52 inches; Rear track, 52 inches; Overall length, 155 inches; Overall width, 68 inches; Height to top of screen, 31 inches; Weight less fuel, 1,300lbs distributed 40 per cent/60 per cent front to rear.

M6B The M6B was the 1968 production version of the Championship-winning 6A and differed very little from the original. It was offered by Trojan as a rolling chassis complete with transmission, mountings and exhausts ready to fit a Chevrolet V8 engine and was in tremendous demand. A total of 28 were built and their specifications were virtually identical to the M6A.

M6GT Following the M6-series Group 7 successes, a coupé Group 4 model was projected for the 1969 season. Unfortunately the type met with various problems barring homologation in the class and the project was shelved. The prototype was sold to English privateer David Prophet who ran it with Chevrolet engines of various sizes and later converted it to open specification with a 6B-type body-shell. Another was finished as a high-performance road car for Bruce McLaren's use, and acted as the prototype of a road car series which has yet to be produced.

M7A Robin Herd's was again the guiding hand behind this model's design, as the team's first Cosworth-Ford V8-powered Formula 1 contender. Three M7A monocoques were built for the 1968 season, to be driven by Bruce and Denny Hulme. They were bath-tub type monocoques in the interests of accessibility, and terminated behind the rear cockpit bulkhead, using the engine's crankcase as a fully-stressed rear chassis member.

CHASSIS Monocoque with light aluminium-alloy panelling over steel bulkheads using the engine as a stressed section aft of the cockpit and carrying rear suspension loads though a yoke over the gearbox and plates bolted beneath it.

SUSPENSION Single top link with radius arm, bottom wishbone, anti-roll bar and outboard coil-spring dampers at front. Single top link, reversed lower wishbones, twin radius arms and coil-spring dampers rear. Cast magnesium McLaren wheels 15-inch × 10-inch front and 15-inch × 15-inch rear.

BRAKES Lockheed 17/3P calipers with 11.66-inch diameter discs all round.

BODY Detachable glass fibre nose cone with separate top panel and cockpit surround. Engine cover sometimes used with wings and various spoiler arrangements.

ENGINE Cosworth-Ford DFV V8 mated to five-speed Hewland DG300 transaxle.

DIMENSIONS Wheelbase, 94 inches; Front track, 58 inches; Rear track, 57 inches; Overall width at cockpit, 28 inches; Weight, 1,140lbs.

M7B Starting life as M7A-3, this chassis was fitted with broad pannier tanks at the beginning of 1969 as a research vehicle to test weight distribution and give room for the adoption of a four-wheel drive system. It was not very successful and was sold to Colin Crabbe's Antique Automobiles concern for Vic Elford to drive. He put up some excellent performances in the car before writing it off completely when involved in a shunt with Andretti in the German GP. Apart from the panniers its specification was little different to the more standard M7As.

M7C While the M7A-type bath-tub chassis were tough and accessible they lacked some of the torsional rigidity achieved in the 1969 Formula A/5,000 cars when they appeared. Consequently one F1 car was built using a full 'up-and-over monocoque chassis identical to the M10A 5-litre cars and this machine – known as M7C-1 – became Bruce's personal car in 1969 F1 events. In general specification it was similar to the 'pure' F1 cars.

M7D McLaren Racing came to an agreement with Autodelta early in 1970 to build a chassis to accept one of their 3-litre Alfa Romeo T33 V8 engines. This new chassis followed the two-year-old M7-series design but was 2 inches longer in the wheelbase (at 96-inches) to accommodate the Italian engine.

M8A These 1968 works CanAm cars were further developments of the successful M6A design and were again kept as simple as possible, using single-curvature panelling and square tube sections in the monocoque. This now used the engine as a partially-stressed structural member, and three were built. Bruce and Denny dominated the Championship once again, and Denny took the title.

CHASSIS Aluminium-alloy and magnesium panelled monocoque based on steel bulkheads and using the Chevrolet engine as a partially-stressed structural member stiffening the rear bay.
SUSPENSION Single top link with radius arm, lower wishbone, anti-roll bar and coil-spring dampers at front. Twin radius arms with single top link, reversed lower wishbone and coil-spring dampers at rear. McLaren cast magnesium wheels all round, 15-inch × 10-inch front and 15-inch × 15-inch rear.
BRAKES Lockheed discs all round, 12-inch diameter with 17/3P calipers and dual hydraulic circuits.
BODY Formed by the monocoque sides with detachable glass fibre upper panels and aerodynamic surfaces.
ENGINE Chevrolet V8 mated to four-speed Hewland LG500 transaxle.
DIMENSIONS Wheelbase, 94 inches; Front track, 57.6 inches; Rear track, 56 inches.

M8B Three new and further developed works Group 7 cars were built for the 1969 CanAm series, using at least one of the original 8A monocoques. They differed from the earlier cars in body design – using high-mounted wings standing above the tail on suspension-mounted struts – and had new 7-litre engines built by George Bolthoff, an ex-Traco engineer who had replaced Gary Knutson in the team. There were minor detail differences between the 8Bs and the earlier 8As, and they also used larger wheels – 15-inch × 11-inch fronts and 15-inch × 16-inch rears. They were unbeaten in CanAm events and Bruce took his second Championship title.

M8C This model was the 1970 production version of the all-conquering M8-series design, but differed in some important respects. It was felt that private customers would wish to fit engines other than the Chevrolet ZL-1s used by the works, and rear-bay cross-members were provided to support optional engines, replacing the subframes used to stress the blocks in the 8A and 8B models. Specification was otherwise similar to the earlier models and demand was high, Trojan building 15 cars.

M8D Three new cars were assembled for the 1970 CanAm championship, and were again improvements on the basic theme. Strut-mounted wings acting on the suspension were no longer allowed and the 8D used separate aerofoil sections mounted on tall fins on either rear wing. These earned the cars the name of 'Batmobile' and with 7.5 litre engines built in Livonia, Detroit, by Bolthoff they were again successful, Hulme winning another CanAm title. Bruce was killed while testing the original M8D at Goodwood. Specifications were as for the earlier 8-series cars but for front track of 62.3 inches; rear track, 58.5 inches; overall length, 164 inches; weight, 1,420lbs. A Hewland LG600 four-speed transaxle was now fitted.

M9A In common with Cosworth, Lotus and Matra, McLaren Racing developed a four-wheel drive Formula 1 car during the

1969 season. Basis of the car was a simple twin-boom mono-coque, with the Cosworth-Ford engine turned back-to-front and driving forward to a McLaren-designed 4wd transmission. The gearbox was just behind the driver's seat with drive shafts going to tiny limited slip differentials at front and rear along the left side of the car. Despite extensive testing the car was only raced once, and in common with the other 4wd projects was soon abandoned.

CHASSIS Twin boom aluminium skinned monocoque formed over steel bulkheads and terminating aft of the cockpit. Engine supported by a tubular subframe also providing pick-ups for the rear suspension.

SUSPENSION Upper rocker arm operating inboard coil-spring dampers, lower link with radius arm and anti-roll bar at front. Upper rocker arm operating inboard coil-spring dampers, reversed lower wishbone, twin radius arm and anti-roll bar at rear. McLaren cast magnesium wheels, 13-inch × 12-inch front and 13-inch × 14-inch rear.

BRAKES Girling 12-inch diameter ventilated discs at front and rear, mounted inboard to reduce unsprung weight.

BODY Formed by monocoque sides with detachable glass fibre nose cone, cockpit surround and aerodynamic surfaces.

ENGINE Cosworth-Ford DFV 3-litre V8 driving to McLaren-designed and built four-wheel drive transmission with torque split integral with gearbox.

DIMENSIONS Wheelbase, 95 inches; Front track, 59 inches; Rear track, 59 inches; Overall width at cockpit, 36 inches; Weight, 1,160lbs.

M10A McLaren were one of comparatively few major manu-facturers to produce a Formula A/5,000 chassis when the class was introduced to Europe in 1969. Trojan put the model into production and while it was based on Formula 1 design experience there was an interesting feed-back in the M7C F1 car described above. The M10As were extremely successful and dominated the first year of European Formula 5,000. Trojan built 17 cars that first season.

CHASSIS Full 'up-and-over' monocoque with aluminium-alloy panelling bonded and riveted to fabricated steel bulk-heads. Rearward-extending pontoons supported the engine.

SUSPENSION Single top link with radius arm, lower wishbone, anti-roll bar and outboard coil-spring dampers at front. Single top link, reversed lower wishbone, twin radius arms and out-board coil-spring dampers at rear. McLaren cast magnesium wheels all round, 15-inch × 11-inch front and 15-inch × 16-inch rear (10.55 × 15 and 12.50 × 15 tyres).

BRAKES Lockheed ventilated discs all round with LA4-24 calipers.

BODY Formed by monocoque sides with detachable glass fibre nose cone-cum-cockpit surround and optional aerofoil spoiler.

ENGINE 5-litre (305 cubic inch) Chevrolet V8 as standard, mated to Hewland LG600 five-speed transaxle.

DIMENSIONS Wheelbase, 98 inches; Front track, 59 inches; Rear track, 60½ inches; Overall length, 157½ inches; Overall width, 77 inches; Height to top of screen, 26½ inches; Weight (less fuel), 1,285lbs.

M10B The 1970 development of the production FA/5,000 car differed from the original in several respects. The steering geometry was revised with low-offset front wheels, and the engine bay was altered to lower the engine mounting by 2-inches. The rear top-beam and its suspension pick-ups was also dropped, and a DG300 gearbox replaced the original LG600 unit, saving considerable weight. Dimensions and specifications were otherwise similar to the earlier car, and Peter Gethin won his second consecutive Guards F5,000 championship title with one of the 21 M10Bs Trojan produced.

M11 Designation not used due to likely confusion with 'Mark II'.

M12 This was an out-of-sequence classification applied to the 1969 production Group 7 sports-racer, which used an M8-type body on a monocoque similar to the M6-series cars. Standard mountings were provided for Chevrolet engines and a total of 15 cars were produced, including one with the narrower M6-type body-shell for hill-climber Phil Scragg. Chaparral Cars ran one M12 for John Surtees while their own 2G model was being developed.

CHASSIS Monocoque with aluminium-alloy panelling bonded and riveted to fabricated steel bulkheads, with three fuel cells in the sills and under the driver's knees holding 52 gallons.

SUSPENSION Unequal length wide-based wishbones, anti-roll bar and coil-spring dampers at front. Single top links and reversed lower wishbones with twin radius arms and coil-spring dampers. McLaren cast magnesium wheels all round, 15-inch × 10-inch front and 15-inch by 15-inch rear (10.55 × 15 and 1.50 × 15 tyres).

BRAKES Girling ventilated discs, 12-inch diameter front and rear, with 16-3-LA calipers and dual hydraulic circuits.

BODY Formed by monocoque sides with detachable glass fibre top panels.

ENGINE Mountings as standard for Chevrolet V8 mated to Hewland LG five-speed transaxle.

DIMENSIONS Wheelbase, 93½ inches; Front track, 57 inches; Rear track, 55 inches; Overall length, 155 inches; Overall width, 75 inches; Height to top of screen, 30 inches; Weight (less fuel), 1,300lbs distributed 40 per cent/60 per cent front to rear.

M13 Designation not allocated.

M14A Three of these 1970 Formula 1 cars were built at the start of the season and the design team of Bruce McLaren, Gordon Coppuck and Jo Marquart had made several important innovations. Most notable of these was the adoption of inboard rear brakes in an effort to save unsprung weight.

CHASSIS Full monocoque with aluminium and magnesium panelling bonded to fabricated steel bulkheads, terminating behind the rear cockpit bulkhead and using the engine as a fully-stressed chassis member.

SUSPENSION Single top link with radius arm, lower wishbone, anti-roll bar and outboard coil-spring dampers at front. Single-top link, reversed lower wishbone, twin radius arms and outboard coil-spring dampers at rear. McLaren cast magnesium wheels all round, 15-inch × 11-inch fronts and 15-inch × 16-inch rears.

BRAKES Lockheed ventilated discs all round, 11.66 inches diameter fronts and 10.90 inches diameter rears mounted inboard.

BODY Formed by monocoque sides with glass fibre detachable nose cone and cockpit surrounds.

ENGINE Cosworth-Ford DFV 3-litre V8 mated to Hewland DG300 five-speed transaxle.

DIMENSIONS Wheelbase, 95 inches; Front track, 62.4 inches; Rear track, 60 inches; Overall length, 156 inches; Weight, 1,180lbs.

M14D This was a one-off Formula 1 chassis built halfway through the 1970 season to accept an Alfa Romeo V8 engine. It was similar to the Cosworth-Ford engined cars in all respects apart from a 2-inch increase in wheelbase (to 97-inches) to accommodate the larger engine.

M15A 1970 saw McLaren's first attack on the Indianapolis 500, and the team built three new cars closely based on the simple and effective CanAm designs. Sponsorship came from Goodyear, Gulf Oil and Reynolds Aluminium, and with turbocharged Offenhauser four-cylinder engines the three M15s proved extremely competitive in early testing. Sadly Denny was burned when his car caught fire in qualifying and Chris Amon found he could not work up to competitive speeds. Peter Revson and Carl Williams took over the two race cars, Revson retiring with mechanical failure and Williams finishing ninth.

CHASSIS Broad aluminium-alloy panelled monocoque formed

over steel and aluminium bulkheads, with the engine acting as a semi-stressed member in the rear bay.

SUSPENSION Single top link with radius arm, lower wishbone, anti-roll bar and outboard coil-spring dampers with adjustable ride height at front. Single top link, reversed lower wishbone, twin radius arms, anti-roll bar and outboard coil-spring dampers at rear. McLaren cast magnesium wheels all round with knock-off hub nuts, rims 15-inch × 10-inch fronts and 15-inch × 14-inch rears.

BRAKES Lockheed ventilated discs all round, 11.97 inches diameter.

BODY Formed by monocoque sides with detachable glass fibre upper panelling forming the nose cone-cum-cockpit surround, engine cover and chassis-mounted aerofoil. Side sponsons carry 67 US gallons fuel.

ENGINE 2.6 litre four-cylinder turbocharged Offenhauser mated to a Hewland LG500 four-speed transaxle, modified with provision for external starting.

DIMENSIONS Wheelbase, 98$\frac{11}{16}$ inches; Front track, 57$\frac{3}{4}$ inches; Rear track, 58$\frac{1}{16}$ inches; Width at cockpit, 45 inches; Overall length, 156 inches; Weight, 1,380lbs distributed 70 per cent/30 per cent front to rear.

M16A This is the wedge-shaped Indianapolis car for 1971 using the turbocharged Offenhauser engine and a Hewland LG transaxle. The chassis is a full aluminium monocoque with Goodyear fuel bags. Wheelbase is 101-inches, with front and rear track 58 inches. Wheels are 15-inch diameter front and rear with 10-inch front rims and 14-inch rear rims. Front suspension is by rocker arm and lower wishbone, and rear suspension is by reversed lower wishbone with a top link and radius rods. The M16A also uses Koni shock absorbers, Lockheed brakes, McLaren rack and pinion steering, Hewland driveshafts, Borg & Beck clutch and a Marston Excelsior radiator.

M17   Designation allocated to 3-litre prototype sports car but project abandoned.

M18A   Formula A/5,000 car for 1971 using a 5-litre Chevrolet V8 engine with a Hewland DG transaxle. It has a full aluminium monocoque chassis with a wheelbase of 100-inches, front track of 59.5 inches and rear track of 60 inches. It has 13-inch front wheels with 11-inch rims and 15-inch rear wheels with 16-inch rims. Front suspension is by a lower wishbone with a top link and radius arm, while the rear suspension is by a reversed lower wishbone with a top link and radius rods.

M19A   Formula 1 car for 1971 using the Cosworth-Ford DFV V8 engine with a Hewland DG transaxle. The car has a 'coke bottle' shape not unlike the Tyrrell-Ford driven by Jackie Stewart in 1970. It has an aluminium monocoque with a wheelbase of 100 inches, front track of 63 inches, and rear track is 62 inches. Front wheels are 13 inches in diameter with 10-inch rims and the rear wheels are 3 inches in diameter with 16-inch rims. Rising rate suspension all-inbourd with cantilevers and rocker arms. Weight is 1,230 lbs. Koni shock absorbers are used, McLaren rack and pinion steering, Lockheed brakes, a Borg & Beck clutch, and Hewland or BRD driveshafts.

M8E   The Trojan production CanAm sports car for 1971 based on the prototype tested briefly by Denis Hulme at Goodwood in 1970. It has the basic shape of the M8B with a low wing instead of the side fins of the works M8D. The track is narrower than the works M8D, and the car has a smaller fibreglass body. The wheelbase is 95 inches with a front track of 58 inches and rear track of 55.5 inches. Wheels are 15-inch diameter with 11-inch front rims and 16-inch rear rims.